The Business Pilgrim's Progress

From a World of Mediocrity towards the Land of Prosperity

HOW TO GIVE BETTER-THAN-EXCELLENT SERVICE AND RECEIVE GREATER-THAN-EXPECTED REWARDS

Colin Turner

coronet

CORONET BOOKS

Hodder & Stoughton

First published in Great Britain in 2000
by Hodder and Stoughton
First published in paperback in 2001
by Hodder and Stoughton
A division of Hodder Headline

A Coronet Paperback

10 9 8 7 6 5 4 3 2 1

A CIP catalogue record for this title
is available from the British Library.

ISBN 0 340 72893 0

Printed and bound in Great Britain by
Mackays of Chatham PLC, Chatham, Kent

Hodder and Stoughton
A division of Hodder Headline
338 Euston Road
London NW1 3BH

CONTENTS

Chapter One

Leaving the City of Apathy

Put by the curtains,
Look within my veil;
Turn up my metaphors, and do not fail:
There if thou seekest them such things to find,
As will be helpful to an honest mind.

John Bunyan

This is the story of one man's pilgrimage from the City of Apathy, in the State of Mediocrity, where he lived and worked. He wanted to seek out a better place, a Land of Prosperity, where what a person does always expresses, and constantly fulfils, their true potential.

As Chris, for that is the name of our pilgrim, allowed me the opportunity to chronicle his progress, it falls upon me to share with you his incredible trials and tribulations. Experiences that led him, and the companions who joined him, to learn, understand and apply the Enlightened level of Service essential to gain entry to Service City, wherein the King, Customer, reigned.

According to the State of Mediocrity's definition of success,

Chris was a shining example. He had done what had been expected of him at school and earned an average degree at university. In the ten years that followed he had worked for a reasonably reputable company, had married and had been blessed with two children.

Because of his youthful zest for life, his skill of dealing with people and his ability to work hard he had recently been appointed Sales and Marketing Director for his firm, Communication Limited. But it was at this point that he began to feel increasingly burdened with a gnawing sense of frustration and it is here that our story begins.

'Take a seat,' commanded Receptionist robotically, with a cursory glance before returning to scan the monitor of her computer. 'I'll be with you in a minute.' Her second glance to confirm her instructions had been carried out turned to one of horror, as she could not believe her eyes. 'Excuse me! What on earth do you think you are doing?'

Chris was not sure what had come over him, perhaps it was the final straw in a whole series of recent events that had cast doubts on the society he was living in. But at that moment he had decided to follow Receptionist's instruction precisely. He had literally picked up one of the chairs in the waiting area and begun to walk out with it. 'Ah!' said Chris, 'At last I have your attention. I was wondering what someone has to do to be served.'

Receptionist's eyes narrowed. She may have been caught off guard but there was no way she was going to allow *anyone* to query the autocracy with which she clearly ruled her domain. 'This is a Legal Department,' she answered slowly, 'we don't serve, we sue.'

What is it about certain receptionists, thought Chris. Isn't it their job to welcome people and then direct them on to the right place? He noticed the handsomely-framed Mission Statement that was hanging on the wall. The meaningful message was highly commendable and, like his own company's, had probably taken many hours to evolve. Yet the part: *committed to serve our clients*, seemed incongruous with Receptionist's behaviour. She was the 'shop window' of the office, the point of first call, a client's first experience of the company she represented. Had she bought into what was hanging on the wall? Had she even been involved in its creation? Perhaps the answer was in the second part of that statement: *to the best of our abilities*. People's best abilities had obviously not been fully developed here. Or was it Chris? Perhaps *their* attitude was right and it was *him* that was being difficult.

Over the past two weeks Chris had been focusing increasingly on the way he was served, in many different kinds of situations. He was trying to work out whether those people who had served him had actually enjoyed the opportunity to be of service. Perhaps even liked him. He had come to the conclusion that they served because they *had* to, because it was their job. Not because they wanted to, or chose to, let alone *enjoyed* it.

'So, do you *have* an appointment?' asked Receptionist forcing herself to be pleasant, while once more scanning her screen in anticipation for the automated answer. The one that should now come her way, as it always did from people who entered her domain. Chris dutifully obliged with a ritual of precise answers providing what Receptionist *must* know, details that he knew would be on the screen in front of her. He did, however, notice a clear change in her tone and demeanour when she realised that it was a Senior Partner he was visiting, and that they were having lunch together.

'Take a se … I'll let Lawyer know that you are here … you shouldn't have to wait long.'

Why should Receptionist become more pleasant because of *who* he was seeing, thought Chris. What difference should that make? Yet clearly it made her more amenable to him. Or was she more concerned that Chris would report the exchange to her boss *before* she did.

'You'll like this restaurant,' said Lawyer. 'It's very exclusive, you know, and the food is excellent.'

'And the service too, no doubt,' replied Chris.

'Eh? Yes of course – particularly if you're a regular patron. You go in and I'll join you in a moment, just got to wash my hands.'

Chris walked up to the reservation gate and stood by the sign: 'wait to be seated'. Why couldn't it read 'please wait to be greeted', or 'please let us guide you to your table', at least something more welcoming, thought Chris. A moment later Maître D' appeared and asked Chris his name, rank and number, to which Chris responded obediently, although reluctantly. By now Chris had realised that to do anything other than 'as he was told' would compromise what Maître D' saw as the security of his position and probably delay lunch.

During the meal Chris occasionally watched the waiters, particularly when other diners were attempting to catch their waiter's attention – or any waiter for that matter. He noticed that some of the waiters had mastered the art of busily ignoring the desperate customer who wanted to attract their attention. Their job was to take a particular dish to a specific table, so they really did not want to be waylaid, especially if the table was not within their specified area. They almost seemed to sense when a diner wanted to get their attention, and become even more elusive. Surely it was not possible to avoid gazes, in the way that they did, without consciously trying? For the second time that day Chris wondered if the staff had chosen to work here, were forced into it, or were simply waiting for something else to come up. It was quite clear to see which waiters enjoyed what they did, those that did not and the ones who were just biding their time.

'You seem weighed down with the world's problems, anything bothering you?' enquired Lawyer.

'Do you ever phone your own office?' asked Chris as if in reply.

'Eh? What do you mean? Of course I do, doesn't everyone some time or other?' answered Lawyer, puzzled.

'I mean the main number, the same one that your clients have to phone?'

'Of course not,' he retorted. 'If I need to speak to anyone, or get messages I simply phone my assistant on her direct line, same as you do, no doubt.'

'And leave a message on her voice mail?' enquired Chris further.

'If she's not there, which is more often than not the case, come to think of it, since we had the system installed by your people,' replied Lawyer.

'But have you *any* idea how your prospective and existing clients are greeted when they first phone or even visit your firm?'

Lawyer looked thoughtful.

Chris did not return to his office immediately after lunch. He needed time to think as his head was pounding with frustration. Perhaps he was worried because, as Sales and Marketing Director, he was directly responsible for his company's future success and his awareness of service had changed. He was becoming more and more conscious that good service was just non-existent. Even the signs in the park through which he was presently walking instructed what you *couldn't* do. No litter, keep off the grass. They never invited what you were *able* to do, like please keep to the paths. In fact, as Chris considered the events of the day he began to realise that all the service he had experienced had been half-hearted and completely without goodwill.

On the way to his lunch appointment he had been forced to take *the* taxi he didn't like the look of. He had gone to the clean non-smoking one, third in line, and had been told that he must take the one at the head of the queue. You're paying for a ride, not the quality of the vehicle, you know, Driver had quipped unpleasantly. The trip had been uncomfortable as Driver had an aggressive attitude to traffic while continually speaking on his mobile telephone. Nearing Chris's destination Driver had said, 'The address is down a one way street so it'll be easier to drop you off here.' Easier for who, thought Chris, me? Why was it that Driver was making out he had done Chris a huge favour, as he looked expectantly for a tip when Chris, the customer, paid the fare? The chances of Chris being obliged to say 'thanks for the ride' were infinitely greater than receiving a 'thanks for your custom'. But then he wasn't a *real* customer, he was only a passenger who was lucky enough to find an empty cab. Yes, he had been taken for a ride, and for how long had he. Why did he feel conditioned to give a tip, even when he didn't feel justified in doing so?

Earlier that morning he had phoned the call centre of Communication Limited – his company. This had been set up to deal with customer complaints. After what seemed an interminable time his call was answered.

'Hello', said Chris, 'that took a long time.'

'Well, we're very busy today, I'm afraid,' replied a voice before adding, 'Do you have a reference number?'

Chris dutifully answered, only to be told that the computers were 'down' today and perhaps Chris could call back later.

'Then why did you ask for my reference number?'

Later, on entering a clothes shop, he had been accosted

immediately with 'Can I help you?' In reply Chris had asked did they really want to.

'It's my job,' came the reply, followed with 'Are you *just* looking?' and accompanied by a look as if Chris were some kind of alien.

Next door he had a different experience. His daughter wanted a mini-disc recorder for her birthday, so he intended to get some information on them and check out the prices. After waiting for a few moments at the counter, he noticed that Assistant was busily attending to a product display by the door. A display obviously intended to attract customers, thought Chris. He could hear two other assistants chatting together, hidden by the partition beyond the counter.

He knew that Assistant had noticed him, but it was apparent that he was hoping to finish what he started. Chris was sure that he heard him mumble, 'How can I be expected to finish this product display to attract customers when I am continually interrupted by them?' Seeing that no one would be coming to Chris's assistance, Assistant got up, looked at Chris, and said, 'Yes.'

'I was wondering if you could tell me the difference between these two disc recorders,' asked Chris.

Assistant looked at both the units and after a few moments pointed at one of them.

'That one's the best. Do you want to see it?'

'Well, I can see it quite clearly from here, but why that one?' enquired Chris.

'Because it's the most expensive,' replied Assistant. 'It'll have a better sound.'

Chris could see that they were different makes, but apart from that they looked identical. 'Why is that exactly?' he asked.

'Don't ask me,' said Assistant, 'I'm only part-time.'

Business is still failing to deliver what it
promises, despite genuine initiatives to boost
growth through customer focused service.

Yes, reflected Chris, he had to conclude that *all* the service he had experienced had been done by people *having* to serve him, not wanting to, or even enjoying the opportunity to do so. Service was a job unsupported by either trade or profession.

'Service stinks!' said Chris out loud in despair.

'Not everywhere,' said a voice.

Chris turned and saw a person standing beside him who introduced himself as Intuition.

'There is a place', Intuition continued, 'where the true meaning of Service is understood. Where giving better-than-excellent service is the only acceptable service available. Where the people understand that in work you may only produce something, but in service you have the opportunity to *become* someone.'

'It is hard to imagine that such a place exists,' said Chris. 'Yet, in my heart I feel that it must. I'm not sure why I believe this, other than a hope that such a place would let me cast off this heavy burden. Regardless of where you go in this city, service is not a priority. Please tell me more about this place that you know.'

'Service City is a place rich in abundance and opportunity. It is a place where everyone is loyal to the King out of choice, not necessity. Here, Customer, for that is the name of their King, rules in contentment because the people are prosperous; and, because the people are prosperous, so is their King. It cannot be otherwise, for a wise sovereign's first duty is to be loyal to his people in recognition and reward for their service. In Service City the streets are a delight to experience.'

'If such a place exists I have no alternative but to find it,' said

Chris, 'but what must I do and which way do I go to experience such streets?'

'The journey ahead is testing and there is much that you will have to overcome about yourself, for it is not possible to judge the state of any street until first your own house is found to be in good order.'

'Reluctantly, I must admit that although I may believe that a better way of service exists, I don't know what I must do in order to gain such knowledge. But I am willing to leave this State of Mediocrity, which I currently live in.'

'Good,' said Intuition, 'for the Land of Prosperity wherein Service City stands can only be entered with a willing heart, though this is not sufficient on its own. Much more is required. Learning, understanding and applying what can only be described as Enlightened Service can only come through greater awareness gained . . .'

'But already I am aware that something is wrong,' interrupted Chris. 'That despite the genuine and sincere initiatives of business to boost profitable growth through greater emphasis and focus on customer services and marketing, they are still failing to deliver what they promise.'

'There are three stages from unawareness to awareness,' said Intuition. 'Most individuals and businesses are first unaware that they are unaware. Then, as you are now experiencing, they become aware that they are unaware. The third, which follows a path consciously chosen, leads to becoming aware that they are aware. This level can only be gained through a personal journey that seeks the development of potential. The marketing initiatives of which you speak, for example, are based on a wrong interpretation of marketing. Rather than ask "*Who* is our customer and *how* can we deliver what they really want?", marketing at the moment asks "how can we sell *more* of what *we* want to sell?" It does fulfil what it was intended for by looking to the customer aspirations to influence strategy. It merely acts as a tool to support sales.'

> Marketing must ask, *who* is our customer and
> *how* can we deliver what they really want?
> Not, *how* can our business sell *more* of what
> we've got.

'I feel that I am being pulled in two directions,' said Chris 'and am at a loss to know which way to turn.'

'It is how you progress through your journey that will allow you to shed your current burden of frustration. If you do not seek that which is in your heart to do then your burden can only increase. Be advised that this City of Apathy will not survive for much longer and their markets will be taken from them. Your initial awareness must therefore be heeded, or your only future will be one of being lost in a State of Mediocrity where the only visitor will be No One. Commence your journey at the Change Border and ask to see Evaluate. Give him this card of mine that I give to you now and request that he assists you. Answer his questions correctly and he will guide you further.'

'Look Chris, I haven't got the time for this,' said his fellow director, Too-Busy, when Chris got back to the office and tried to have a word with him. 'We've done the change thing *and* the mission thing already so I can't see what you're getting so upset about.'

'And, it was expensive,' Cynical interjected. 'I've never been convinced that any of it was worth the amount of money spent on it. Money that *could* have been utilised elsewhere.'

'But *I* don't remember any involvement,' returned Chris. 'And apart from a few redundancies, my department didn't notice any change. We still had to follow the same old processes without question. The only difference is that we had a *statement* for what we aspired to do hanging on the wall.'

'Perhaps you benefited more than you realise,' said Hidden-Agenda. 'After all, you *are* heading your department now, no complaints in that respect, eh?'

'The point that I'm making,' replied Chris, 'is that we must listen to what our customers want and build our policy and strategy around *their* wants.'

'That would be economic suicide!' blurted out Cynical. 'Our strategy is based on offering them what *we* have for sale in such an *attractive* way that *they* go ahead and *buy* it. It works. As Head of Marketing, it's your job to keep making our products attractive.'

'But what we're telling them is *not* what we're selling them,' protested Chris.

'Look, everyone knows that the loudest and most frequent voice sells — that's a first rule of marketing, so who cares? And with our products selling as well as they are, you have a good marketing budget to make certain we stay the most often heard voice, don't you? Anyway they can always contact our New Customer Complaints Desk, can't they,' continued Hidden-Agenda. 'That's a service we specifically set up for them, isn't it?'

'No, it had to be set up to cope with the complaints,' replied Chris. '*That* was the reason. Our policy should be aiming towards fewer complaints, not catering for them. Why can't we aim for zero defects by trying to understand what the customer wants?'

'Zero defects?' said Too-Busy. 'It's just not possible in business today, and the time involved just doesn't bear thinking about. Who expects it anyway?'

'Would *you* take a flight if you thought the mechanics of the aircraft did not check out with zero defects?' asked Chris.

'But how do we know for certain that there are zero defects?' answered Cynical. 'If I pull down the table from the seat in front of me during a flight and there's an old coffee stain there, it makes me think what *oil* stains have gone unnoticed in the engine. But surely the reality of today is that people *accept* that what they are told may not be completely backed up. They accept that what they buy will probably not last, or perform as well as they have been led to believe it will. But at least we're not living in the Victorian Times now, thank God. I would imagine that people working in the service industry today do so for the money, not because they want to. Business is about making profit. And people know that companies are out to make as much as they can. Even if you were successful in developing a strategy for excellent service, let alone better-than-excellent, as you say, how would you get our people to buy into it? To them it would just be another strategy and they would only pay it lip service.'

'Of course business must make profit!' shouted Chris. 'That isn't my point, for making a profit is what business is about. But I believe that profit should be regarded as the applause for providing good acts of service. So, by providing excellent service we will enjoy the reward of greater applause from our audience. That's the reality!'

> Profit is simply the applause for performing
> good acts of service.

'All business, and particularly service-oriented ones like us, are operating under a false illusion,' continued Chris. 'Business has conditioned itself to believe that customers need business. That's getting it backwards. Business needs customers. After all they are the very reason for our existence – without them there would be no revenue, let alone profit! Most people in business do not even know who their prime customer is.'

'So *who* would you consider *yours* to be?' enquired Hidden-Agenda.

'The very people who have to follow the strategy and policy that we formulate,' answered Chris, 'the employees of course.'

'Our *employees*?' said Cynical in surprise. 'What about our shareholders? We certainly wouldn't be here without their support. And what about our *paying* customers? Surely they come *before* those people we pay?'

'Every one of our people should be an ambassador of our business and, as such, has a vital role to perform,' said Chris. 'Every ambassador must have the full support of the ruling nation that it represents. Surely, our duty is to serve them through training, systems, rewards and recognition to the best of our ability so that they in turn can perform with their prime customers, the *paying* ones to coin your phrase, to the best of their ability. Take a ship. When the crew have difficulty with a passenger, and are not certain how to handle them, they seek the captain's advice and support, both in morale and in competency. The captain takes such necessary action that will ensure the safety of the vessel that carries both the crew and passengers.

'The ship's owner must stand by the captain's decision, whatever it may be, because it is the captain's style of leadership that they invested in to obtain the best return. The captain serves his crew best when he is on the bridge overseeing operations, not while he is in his cabin. Any crewmember, *or* passenger, can speak to the captain should either consider it appropriate.'

'Well, I certainly haven't got the time to speak to every employee,' said Too-Busy. 'And the nature of our work is such that I don't have the time to prittle-prattle with customers. For goodness' sake, we have a huge call centre that spends all day communicating with customers. We have a Human Resource

Training and Personnel department for our people. No, I'm sorry, but as far as I'm concerned my prime customers are our major shareholders and with a possible profits warning coming up next quarter I want to keep on the right side of them – we may need extra support.

'Chris, enough of your ideas on better *service*; what we need from you is some marketing ideas for better *sales*.'

'What good will resigning do?' asked Christine later that evening in response to her husband's concerns. 'You've only just got to the position where you can make a difference. It strikes me that you are almost shying away from the responsibility of what's ahead of you.'

'Certainly, the job has opened my eyes to the poor level of service that our customers have to put up with,' agreed Chris, 'but because of the constraints hidden within established processes and policy, the job may as well be in title only. It's responsibility without power, which is ironic because in my experience most people want power without the responsibility that command brings. You know that *that* is not the case with me, Christine, I always honour my commitments. It's just that I feel that I am compromising what I believe to be right, by not delivering what marketing invites and sales promise.'

'Well, I don't want us to lose what we already have, quite frankly. Just because you're all fired up with some foolish notion that some *stranger*, of all people, has put you up to. Anyway, I really don't see what you're so frustrated about. We have a nice home, fine children, friends, a good quality of life – why would you want to risk losing what we have worked so hard for?'

'I don't, but I *do* feel weighed down with a sense of emptiness. I want to feel a greater sense of fulfilment in what I do. It is not that I am *dis*satisfied with my life, but I do feel *un*satisfied. There must be more to life than just *doing* to *getting*. And if you're referring to my meeting with Intuition,' said Chris, 'let me tell you that he seemed more like a long-lost friend than some stranger, as you suggest. His words of guidance made sound sense to me and I believe that by following his advice I will shed this burden that is weighing me down.'

Christine had not seen her husband like this before. Her immediate reaction was to tell him to pull himself together and stop being so stupid, but she managed to stop herself at the last moment. In an instant she went back to her childhood and heard her parents saying the same words to her. Words that she had vowed not to say to her own children if she became a mother. Well, she had become a mother and she had even heard herself saying the same words to her children, despite her vow, and now here she was about to say the same to her husband. She felt a wave of insecurity begin to sweep through her and fought to control it. As she did so it was as if she recognised the waters she had entered. She became certain that they were the same ones that had so often threatened to drown her mother and father.

She remembered her mother being frustrated at having to make ends meet, she remembered her father being frustrated because he felt he was not doing enough. She remembered her own frustration, as a girl, because she was taught to hide her strengths while her brother was encouraged to reveal his. She remembered her brother's frustration because such encouragement was overshadowed by their concern for what he was not good at. Now, before her, her own husband carried a burden of frustration. But he was determined to take action because of it. Should she stand in his way? She may be able to console him, but she could not take the burden away from him. In her heart she accepted that only *he* could do that. But this talk of resigning seemed too drastic. Then an idea came to her.

'Take a holiday,' she said, 'a business holiday.'

'I haven't time for a holiday, and anyway the kids are both at school.'

'I said a business holiday.'

'What do you mean a business holiday? There isn't such a thing.'

'Look, you're always saying that the best ideas are always made out of the office. So, why not undertake a period of Marketing Research specifically to find out about this Enlightened Service you've heard about. If what you have heard is true then everyone will benefit. You'll no longer feel burdened and Communication Limited will enjoy profitable growth.'

Chris looked at his wife while he considered the full importance of what she had just said. The idea seemed like music to his ears. Perhaps because he had been too close to the problem he had been unable to see a way out of his dilemma. But this was perfect. It was ethical and made good sense. A business holiday was a paradox in itself and out of paradoxes came success.

A business holiday is a paradox but out of paradoxes come success.

'That really is a brilliant idea, but how do you feel about me chasing after what most people have said is a crazy dream?'

'Perhaps in listening to you I've realised that if we don't take the opportunity to chase our dreams we end up feeling that something of ourselves is missing.'

It did not take Chris long to organise himself for the trip. Hidden-Agenda did not seem too concerned about Chris's intention to seek further information about how they could increase profits. Moreover, he seemed quite pleased that Chris would be leaving. Cynical had his doubts that whatever Chris returned with, if he did in fact return, would be of any use and Too-Busy ratified the trip only on the basis that Chris took the trip on his own time.

'You're due a holiday, so take it how you want,' he had said. 'Business holiday indeed! I'm sure that market research can be done from the office – which is where you're paid to be after all. Take me, everybody sees me at my desk when they arrive and when they leave. Prove that it works and then we can talk about it *not* being *your* holiday.'

Chris set off in the direction that Intuition had earlier advised, and where he would meet Evaluate at Change Border. He soon noticed two colleagues hurrying after him, Indecisive and Fixed-Thinking.

'So you're really as serious as they say you are?' asked Indecisive. 'What on earth is it that you are so earnestly chasing after, even to the point that you will leave this whole world behind?'

'Yes, I'm absolutely serious,' began Chris, 'it is because this world is so frustrating that I must look for . . .'

'Then you are as crazy as they say you are!' interrupted Fixed-Thinking. 'The grass may appear greener to you elsewhere, but let me tell you, it's just as hard to cut. Our city may be laid back, but who cares, if everyone's content with the way it is?'

'Laid back?' replied Chris, 'This city is more than that! Our service is non-existent and our attitude to service is apathetic. Such a city will not survive in the new era that is coming.'

'What new era?' asked Indecisive.

'A new era of customer-focused service, where customers are discerning, know what they want and will have the power to make or break businesses by their choices.'

'That's ridiculous,' said Fixed-Thinking. 'There will always be customers for the products and services that businesses sell them. Admittedly, some customers are *difficult*, but there are always plenty more to take their place if they don't want to buy. There may be a lot of change and technological advances these days, but people are people and, let me assure you, in this the future is merely an extension of the past.'

'People are not machines,' said Chris, 'they are a life force and as such are continually evolving. And to me it is clear that our sense of awareness is evolving much faster than our physical bodies.

> Today, more than ever before, people are conscious of their ability to accomplish whatever they set their minds to.

'People are becoming increasingly conscious of themselves as powerful thinking individuals with the ability to achieve whatever they set their minds to. People are becoming increasingly more discerning, they want to know that they *count* for something, instead of being just counted as statistics. It is my belief that the best way to serve yourself is through serving others but, because I do not know how to go about such a thing, I am embarking on a learning journey that leads to Service City in the Land of Prosperity. Why don't you both accompany me?'

'Accompany you?' repeated Fixed-Thinking with a hint of contempt in his voice. 'No way! I'm going to keep my feet firmly on this ground that I know. It stops your head from staying in the clouds where some people insist on being. I'm off! Serving *others* indeed, whatever next?' and pulling Indecisive to one side he added, 'Being in the company of him will not do us any good – his days are numbered. Come on.'

Indecisive paused and said, 'No, I'm not sure. Perhaps our colleague could be on to something here. What if this place he knows about *does* offer better opportunity and rewards? I've lived and worked in our State of Mediocrity all my life so I have nothing to lose by seeing the alternative.'

'Humph! *If* this place exists!' retorted Fixed-Thinking. 'Just because you're still all fired up from that training course you went on last week you're not seeing things the way they really are. But *don't* worry, you'll soon get back to normal, everyone always does. So, go on, off you go. I have no doubt that I'll see you later,' and Fixed-Thinking stormed off.

'Well,' said Indecisive turning back to Chris, 'I'm with *you*, for the moment. Where do we go from here?'

'We must first make our way beyond the city outskirts and go directly to the Change Border,' answered Chris. 'There we are to gain a pass from Evaluate.'

'So,' said Indecisive excitedly, 'now that there are just the two of us, tell me more of this Land of Prosperity, how soon do you think we'll get there?'

'Everything you've said this morning about Service City makes me long to be there, but let us now stop a while. It's so hot and I'm thirsty. Let's take a break over there.' Indecisive pointed in the direction of a large building, which was absolutely teeming with people eating and drinking. It was the Pub of Procrastination.

'But I told you that Intuition advised me to go directly to Change Border,' said Chris. 'It can't be much further now.'

'You said that ages ago, come on we deserve a quick break.'

Despite having started his pilgrimage, Chris still felt weighed down with his Burden of Frustration so, offering little resistance, he soon found himself seated at a table with Indecisive.

'We're in luck,' said Indecisive joining him with a couple of drinks. 'They'd just stopped serving food, but I managed to persuade them to get us something. I wasn't sure what you'd want, so I left it to them to give us whatever was easiest.'

'Lucky,' snapped Chris, 'but this is an *eating* establishment and it's still lunchtime. Do you mean we can't even choose what we want?'

'Well, I spoke to the barman and he said they're short staffed today. He was actually hoping to finish early today himself, as he had such a late night last night. Anyway, if we don't mind waiting he'll see what he can sort out.'

Chris looked at the ashtray taking pride of place in the table in front of him, its unsightly contents having spilled over to join the variety of drink stains that had also been overlooked. He felt annoyed that he had not noticed the mess immediately as his jacket elbow was now stained as well. Given the choice, he liked to eat and drink off a clean table. Furthermore, although he had nothing against smoking, he would have preferred to be in a non-smoking area. Yet, he noticed that the empty non-smoking area was cordoned off.

'I asked about that when I first came in,' said Indecisive anticipating Chris. 'Apparently, they're expecting a large party this evening and they have to get it ready.'

Chris's thoughts shot to a previous weekend when he had taken his children to a fast food restaurant. The non-smoking area there had also been cordoned off in preparation for a child's birthday party.

The counter where Chris had been queuing had been closed upon the arrival of the party guests as the assistant manager, serving his queue, had to leave to cater for their order.

Swapping to another assistant, as shouted to do so, his waiting time was prolonged while, this time, the trainee assistant, was uncertain of his till and seemed to be pushed aside by colleagues in their rush to fulfil their own orders. 'Fries will take a few minutes,' Chris heard as he watched the existing mound being whisked away to fulfil the ravenous party's order. 'Normally we'd bring them to your table, but just come back and shout, I'll recognise you.'

When Chris commented that perhaps it would be better to wait the assistant had looked at him as if he were an alien. Customers were not meant to confuse staff by making comments. They should only reply to specific questions that would satisfy the demands of the cash register's buttons.

When fully 'trayed-up' for eating in, Chris looked for his children who had gone to find a seat. He spotted them in a corner sitting by a table that was covered in used cartons. Chris noticed that another assistant with a cloth was busy talking to someone at another table, who was clearly a friend.

'We would have tidied up ourselves Dad,' said his children, 'but we didn't want to lose our seat. It took us ages to get this one.'

After their meal Chris took his tray of empties towards one of the disposal bins provided. He had been surprised though, during his meal, at how many people just left their seats without clearing away. If the majority of us are not even prepared to serve ourselves, thought Chris, what hope is there for giving service to others, let alone expecting it?

'It's busy in here today,' Chris had said to the table-clearing assistant, as he deposited his tray's rubbish.

'Tell me about it,' came the reply, 'and no one clears up after themselves like they're meant to. How they expect me to do it all I don't know.'

'Perhaps they think you're there to do it for them,' suggested Chris.

Again Chris was looked at as if he were from another planet. 'No, my job is to clean the tables, not *clear* them. That's the customer's job. But because I'm always doing their job, I never have time to do mine.'

Chris had left the restaurant wondering why he had paid a surcharge to eat in. Would he have had to return and shout for his 'fries' if it had been a take-out?

'There's nothing we can do other than wait,' said Indecisive, bringing Chris back from his reverie. 'We may as well, since we've ordered. Let's have another drink in the meantime – your round I believe.'

'Perhaps it may help if we shout,' said Chris, getting up.

Having eventually caught the attention of one of the barmen, though not to the point that he stopped chatting to the other barman while serving him with his drinks, Chris was able to request a cloth and enquire about their food.

'Food orders have finished today, we're short staffed.'

'Yes, I understand that,' said Chris, 'but I believe that someone is preparing something?'

'Not that I know of. Who did you speak to?'

'It was my colleague who ordered, apparently he paid at the same time.'

'Well, I can't help you till I know who you spoke to, because they shouldn't have taken your order.' And turning to his fellow barman he said, 'Did you take an order for *something*?'

'Food orders have finished today, we're short staffed.'

'Yes, I've told him that, but he's already paid.'

'What did he order?'

'Fries?' volunteered Chris, his recent experience still fresh in his mind.

'Oh,' said the second barman, 'I noticed a bowl of fries on the counter a while ago.'

'Well, perhaps they're ours, though I didn't hear anyone shout,' said Chris.

'*Well*,' said the first barman, as if in imitation of Chris, 'don't look at me, it's hardly my fault.'

Chris took the now cold food and warm drinks back to the table where Indecisive was talking to a person who had joined the table.

'Ah, here you are,' said Indecisive, immediately putting a couple of fries in his mouth. 'Let me introduce you to Complacent. Apparently, he's a regular here and has *never* heard of Change Border.' Not seeming to notice the temperature of the food he added, 'And Complacent doesn't think we're on the right road at all.'

'Not at all,' put in Complacent. 'I've lived in this State all my life and been coming here for as long as I can remember and no one has ever asked me where such a place is.'

'Perhaps Fixed-Thinking had a point,' commented Indecisive. 'He told us that we were dreaming.'

'Ah, dreams,' said Complacent, 'I've spoken to many travellers about their *dreams*. Fortunately I have been able to put them right about such misplaced illusions. Would you believe that one person even shared with me her idea of living in some Land called Prosperity! I said to her, I said, that's not for the likes of you and I. I told her, in no uncertain terms, that to live in such a Land could *only* happen if you were born into it, had the right education, some special talent or knew people in the right places. You ask anyone in here, they'll tell you the same thing.'

Indecisive looked accusingly at Chris, 'But I thought anyone could get into this Land?'

'Well, my advice is to not get your hopes up,' continued Complacent, 'and certainly take the time to think about whether you're doing the right thing. Just think of the hassle ahead of you! Have another drink and relax. After all, if it really exists, and I'm not saying it does, it will still be there tomorrow.'

'How could you have led me astray?' said Indecisive, while Complacent went to refill their glasses. 'Surely you're not expecting me to continue now that our destination is in so much doubt? We ought to have made certain about where we were going before we gave up what we had – I might have lost all that I had by following you.'

'But I *am* certain about our destination,' said Chris who was surprised at how doubtful he sounded to himself. 'I should not have allowed you to distract me from my resolve to leave this city.'

'You ought to be thanking me instead of blaming me,' retorted Indecisive. 'If it weren't for me we would be completely lost by now! At least we've found out *your* error before it is too late!' Pausing he saw that Complacent had not bothered to return as he had said he would. He had joined another table where Indecisive was certain that he was sharing the stupidity of the strangers he had just been talking to. They certainly all seemed very amused.

Indecisive imagined how everyone would laugh at him when he returned from following Chris and his ideas. He would tell them that he had done so only to learn more of Chris's ridiculous ideas for a laugh. But they would not believe him at first, he thought, not until he had derided Chris, and his ideas, for a while. 'I was stupid to listen to you and not Fixed-Thinking,' he continued. 'This is not going to do me any good at all, you and your *Service* City. There's no such place and, as far as *I'm* concerned, there is no need for it anyway. I'm going back and, if you had any sense, you would too.'

When one person's actions point out another's inaction, the latter feels insecure.

Left alone and with one drink following another Chris soon felt disoriented in his thinking. He swayed from thinking what a fool he had been in sharing his intentions with acquaintances, to an immense frustration at being stuck in the rut that he felt he was in. Intuition had warned him not to share with others what was really important to him, until he had found his own path. 'They will only seek your Achilles' heel and use your desires against you, by making fun of them,' he had advised. 'It will be easy for them because you are still not entirely sure of yourself, and uncannily they will just know it. Keep your own counsel.'

The longer he stayed where he was the more he became aware of how hard it was to get started again. Perhaps it was the lack of food against the amount of drink, but a sense of futility for his intended journey weighed him down. Lacking in motivation, it took all of his remaining will power to force himself to one of the Pub of Procrastination's exits. In his 'melancholic' state he first felt himself falling, then caught.

'You look as if you've had a little too much,' consoled Support as she guided Chris out of the sluggish and complacent atmosphere. 'Here, a bit of fresh air is what you need. It will soon get you back on your feet.'

'Thank you,' said Chris. 'You're right, it was difficult to breathe in there.'

'Such air can be insidiously debilitating,' replied Support. 'Certain atmospheres can be as harmful as drugs. And, unwittingly, we can easily become addicted to them. I am not from these parts but have indeed heard of this infamous place. It is said that many have allowed their dreams to dissolve into nothingness from too long an exposure to the Pub of Procrastination. And, like any addiction, they seem unable to stop themselves from returning here on a regular basis.'

The company you keep, like the air you breathe, affects your physical and mental well being.

'How can such a place as this pub continue to exist?' asked Chris, beginning to feel revived. Sharing his ideas with Fixed-Thinking, Indecisive and Complacent and being almost stuck in the Pub of Procrastination had taken its toll on him. He felt vulnerable.

'Because Mankind unwittingly created a society where he is comfortable with average and anyone suggesting higher aspirations is frowned upon as being difficult.'

'But surely there are different levels of societies?' asked Chris.

'Yes, but all are founded on what offers the most security. That is the normal for the majority of those that make up a particular society. The individuals who seek to improve themselves inevitably threaten the status quo, because they highlight the inadequacies in the rest of society. When one's actions points out another's inaction, the latter feels insecure. To feel secure all must follow the same suit. Even the vagabond, who tries to leave the group of vagabonds, is threatened for trying to be someone they believe he is not. "What makes you think you are better than us?" is the cry as they deride him for trying to be different. If, through his efforts, he is fortunate enough to raise his station, he is at first resented, then begrudgingly respected for doing so, then, and not always, his path is followed because he has shown it can be done.'

Chris thought of the resentment of some of his colleagues when he had been promoted. 'I'm better qualified than him,' or 'I've been here longer' were just some of the stories he had heard from the office cubicles he had vacated. 'Better not be seen talking to you now,' one had joked, 'people will think I'm sucking up.' And now, with his ideas on improving service, he knew that many thought 'He's only been in the business for five minutes and he thinks he knows better than us already – who does he think he is?'

'I am determined to seek out a better-than-excellent service,' declared Chris, 'yet everyone I talk to seems determined to talk such an idea down. No one ever wants to see the merits of the possibilities it would bring.'

'People will not see something you want them to, until they are ready, even if what you offer is decidedly in their interests,' said Support. 'Why, I even tried to assist another in a similar situation to yours recently, and he turned on me for trying to help. It was as if he liked the idea of seeking something different, but lacked any initial fortitude to make a start. The Pub of Procrastination got to him more than he realised. He's probably still in there with all his dreams put on hold until another day.'

> Even if what you offer is decidedly in someone's interests, they will not see it until they are ready.

With that, Support said goodbye and the now solitary Chris continued on his way. He had not gone far when, approaching a crossroads, he noticed a well dressed gentleman on his right. Now, unbeknown to our pilgrim at this time, the news of what he was doing had travelled very fast around the State of Mediocrity, as all news frequently does about someone doing something out of the ordinary. This gentleman was Egotist from the town of Mercenary-Policy and he had some specific advice to offer. After initial pleasantries, Egotist asked, 'I hope you don't have to go far with such a heavy burden?'

'As far as is necessary, until I am able to shed it,' replied Chris.

'And where might that be?' enquired Egotist further.

'Towards the Ground of Good Fortune, via Change Border,' answered Chris.

'My goodness,' said Egotist, 'that's a long way and fraught with obstacles, or so I have heard, for few who have travelled there have ever returned to these parts. Why do you not seek an easier route and a place where you can just cast your burden aside?'

'That would be great if there were such a place; losing this burden is on my mind more than anything else.'

'I should think that it is,' said Egotist. 'And your family, no doubt, as well. They must be very concerned about this journey that you have embarked upon?'

'They are indeed, yet there can be no alternative for me to follow.'

'But where did you learn of this alternative, for let me tell you it is not the best one by far,' said Egotist.

'From a man who appeared to me when I felt really lost in the City of Apathy, the city that is now behind me. He appeared to be very sincere.'

'Ah!' said Egotist, 'I have also heard of this man but what I have heard is not good. Not good at all. There is not a more troublesome way in this world than the way that this man has directed you. If you are really in earnest about releasing your burden, then you will not be successful by following his counsel. I can see from the stains on the arm of your jacket that you have already fallen into the Pub of Procrastination. That is just the first of *countless* difficulties that this Intuition's road will lead you into.

'Listen to me, for I am much older than you are and have seen much more of the world. It is better to concentrate on casting aside this burden, rejoining your family and getting on with your life. This road to your left leads to the Village of Instant-Gratification, wherein lies Conformist Court. Make your way there now and ask to meet with High-Regard. Tell him that I sent you and this honest man will help you, in the same way he has eased many others of their burdens. And, when he has, if you still do not feel like returning back to where you lived, there are vacant apartments, which offer everything that you and your family could want.'

Standing at the crossroads Chris wondered whether it would be wise to follow this gentleman's advice. 'How far is it to Conformist Court?' he asked, 'And which way is the quickest?'

'You're not far at all,' replied Egotist. 'Simply follow this road up over that hill and you'll come straight to the village. You can't miss High-Regard's block, as it is the first one you come to.'

So, Chris turned at the crossroads and made his way up the hill towards the Village of Instant-Gratification. Soon, after reaching the top, the road split into two. How strange, thought Chris, they're absolutely identical. Somewhat confused, as this did not entirely match Egotist's directions, he took the first road, only to come upon another fork with two further identical roads. Again he continued and the same thing happened again. 'I can't have gone wrong,' thought Chris, 'as I have certainly not seen any blocks yet, let alone Conformist Court.'

He continued and reached another fork, again with identical roads. 'This is ridiculous,' said Chris out loud to himself. This time he decided to retrace his steps but soon came to another fork. 'How can every road be exactly the same as all the others? Where am I?' There were so many now that it seemed to him in his rising panic that the roads were taking him anywhere rather than leading him somewhere. Chris now started to walk faster, as a person does when feeling lost, in an effort to get out of where they are as quickly as they can.

'Why did I listen to that gentleman? How I wish I were back on the right road!' In his increasing panic, Chris, now exhausted under his heavy burden, ran once more into Intuition.

'What on earth are you doing here?' enquired Intuition.

'This is the Wilderness of Conformity. A place where countless people have lost the *whole* of their lives.'

'I was looking for High-Regard who lives at Conformist Court,' said Chris in anguish.

'Yet, I directed you towards Change Border,' said Intuition. 'Why have you left the path that you were at first so willing to proceed along?'

'I began with good heart,' began Chris, 'but I got bogged down in the Pub of Procrastination. Then, soon after leaving I met a well dressed gentleman who said he knew just who could ease my burden and directed me here.'

> If you take the easy route and just allow
> yourself to be led in different directions, you
> will never follow your true path in life.

'What else did this gentleman say?' asked Intuition.

'He asked where I was going and I recounted that the Ground of Good Fortune was my destination via Change Border. He asked me about my family and work and I answered that I would rather be with my family but having this burden had forced me to seek out better-than-excellent service before I could be content.

'He advised that I look to shedding my burden immediately and directed me to a man who had helped many before to do the same thing and where I would find a place that would bring great contentment for myself and family.'

'This gentleman is most certainly Egotist,' sighed Intuition. 'Both he and High-Regard get their fulfilment from appearing better than others in the world. Both are concerned with their position in society, their credibility and the esteem that others hold them in. Their lives are full of seeking continuous external attractions that in effect only serve to distract them, and the people they counsel, away from their true path. Being from the Town of Mercenary-Policy, this gentleman works only for the sake of himself, never for the sake of others. He regularly visits the Village of Instant-Gratification because he requires such stimulus for his security.

'His friend, High-Regard, purports to ease burdens through offering titles and positions that, in reality, are meaningless. Any ease is short-lived and soon returns with a weightier vengeance. Once someone has followed their advice they can then only reside in Conformist Court where the company is conducive to not feeling out of place.'

'What an idiot I have been,' confessed Chris. 'To be so easily persuaded off my path is a poor sign of my resolve, which I thought so strong.'

'Commitment is not something you can manufacture,' consoled Intuition. 'It is what you discover deep down inside of you when you align what you do with what you are. Commitment therefore must grow and, as it grows, it becomes stronger. But to do so requires it to be tested. The greater you involve yourself with what you are intent upon achieving, the greater your commitment to do what is important to you will grow. And your level of commitment will be as a measure of the strength of your motives for what you do. You will soon see that this is important for you when you arrive at Change Border.

> Commitment is what you discover deep down inside of yourself when you align what you *do* with what you *are*. It is *not* something you can manufacture.

'Now,' continued Intuition, 'look and continue straight ahead of you and this time keep going until you get there. Let your true feelings guide you on the path that providence has planned for you. The way is clear and the first of your goals is just ahead of you. All along the way, however, be aware that distractions will test you, to see if you are really worthy of what you are seeking. Although these distractions are tempting, remember that they are unable to get directly on to your path and stop you. All they can do is distract you on to theirs. Leaving the path is always your choice.'

To Be a Pilgrim ...

- Take action to shed the burden stopping you from releasing your potential
- Know that in work you *produce* something, in service you *become* someone
- Put your own house in order before concerning yourself about the street
- Let your true feelings about what is right guide you on the path that providence has planned
- Know that the best way to serve *yourself* and gain the most reward is through serving *others*
- Gain strength by keeping your own counsel
- Avoid complacent and indecisive people, and procrastination
- Take a business holiday – go on a retreat!

Chapter Two

Visiting Accountability's House

Adhering closely to Intuition's guidance this time, Chris safely arrived at Change Border. He saw that the barrier was closed. There was no sign of anyone to greet him, as he had hoped, but he did notice a written sign above the barrier. It read:

> *All that seek to conceal their motives shall not pass.*
> *Knock only if you are in earnest.*

Chris knocked once, then twice, but no response or assistance seemed forthcoming. After knocking several more times, however, Evaluate appeared before him.

'Welcome to Change Border,' said Evaluate looking directly at Chris. So piercing was the gaze with which he regarded our pilgrim, that Chris was momentarily lost for words. Never before had he experienced such an instantaneous appraisal. It felt as if there was nothing about him that this gaze had not noticed.

'Thank you,' Chris eventually replied. It was all he could think of to say that didn't sound false.

'Why are you here,' asked Evaluate, 'at this time and alone?'

'I was directed to come here by Intuition,' began Chris. 'And you are right, I had hoped to have been here earlier, and was initially accompanied by some colleagues. But here I am now, alone.'

'And exactly as I would have expected, for in truth when we follow our chosen path, everything happens to us at the right time, and in the right place. You have Intuition's card to give me then?'

'Yes indeed,' answered Chris, 'and I am ready to answer the questions that he said you would ask of me.'

'So, I take it that you have chosen to leave this State of Mediocrity behind you of your own free will?' said Evaluate.

'Absolutely,' answered Chris.

'Tell me. How did you assess your colleagues that chose not to accompany you?'

'It was clear to me that one was narrow minded and only heard what he wanted to hear,' said Chris. 'The other lacked fortitude and was prone to allow others to decide for him and then complain when they did so.'

'Did you meet with anyone while coming here and, if so, how did you assess them?' enquired Evaluate.

'Yes, I met with Complacent, who seemed to be comfortable in procrastinating, almost without conscience,' answered Chris, 'and at a crossroads I met with Egotist, who was only out for himself.'

'From your answers it would appear that you are able to recognise the motives of others quite easily,' said Evaluate. 'Am I to understand, therefore, that you did not allow any of them to influence your own actions? Not *even* the likes of Egotist, whose persuasive reputation goes before him?'

Chris felt like an open book under Evaluate's unfailing gaze. 'Well not exactly,' he began. 'I suppose in some way or other they all influenced me to some extent, particularly Egotist, but he seemed so understanding of my plight and I so wanted to let go of this burden I carry.'

'And did his advice ease this burden of yours?'

'Not at all, said Chris. 'In fact, it became heavier and were it not for Intuition guiding me back on the right path, I would have been lost in the Wilderness of Conformity.'

'Please tell me,' asked Evaluate, 'does the nature of your work require you to assess colleagues, customers and generally everyone you meet, on a daily basis?'

'Well yes, of course,' replied Chris.

'So you therefore assess *yourself* on a daily basis?'

'I'm not certain what you mean. Assess myself for what?' said Chris.

'For your own motives of course,' replied Evaluate. 'For it is not possible to assess the motives of another, until first you are able to recognise your own. *Do* you consciously evaluate yourself with regard to your own motives on a daily basis?'

Chris felt uncomfortable. 'No,' he answered truthfully.

'Have you *ever* evaluated yourself with the serious intention of knowing your motives, values and personal ethos?'

'No, I don't believe so,' said Chris quietly.

'Don't be concerned,' consoled Evaluate. 'For although it has become second nature for people to evaluate *others* continuously, either to get a handle on them, or compartmentalise them, it is indeed rare for people to evaluate themselves with the same criteria. Yet it is vital to do so.

First examine your own motives and understand
why you are acting in a particular manner.
Then you can look at others and truly discover
the deeper meaning of their actions.

'When you gain insight into your own actions,' continued Evaluate, 'the behaviour of others becomes clear. There is little point in ensuring that you make all the right moves, when you are unsure of your motives. Yet, when you *are* sure of your motives and in your heart they are clearly right, then the right moves naturally follow. That is why, for example, people are generally reluctant to serve others. In assessing another's motives, while being uncertain, even unaware, of our own, we are in danger of making the wrong moves. Such a thing as serving another is, therefore, perceived as being servile.

'The person who serves another with good heart has motives that are clear to see. Yet the person, who serves another without good heart, has hidden motives. Hidden motives can be used by the holder as a "means" to justify *their perception* of the right "ends".'

Evaluate paused as if remembering something, 'Aversion was such a person who once came by this way. I recall his clear unwillingness to personally offer service to his customers. He felt that dealing directly with them was beneath him, but wanted his sales people to learn how to do so. Yet, the plain truth is we cannot expect others to follow our leadership if we are not prepared to learn and behave first how we expect them to perform.

We cannot expect to be followed if we are not prepared to lead by example.

'The assessments you gave me of your colleagues and the people you met on the road were based on what transpired to you *after* you had allowed yourself to be influenced by them. In recognising their motives *beforehand*, you would have been immune to their adverse influence.'

'But I believe my motives are worthy, so why couldn't I therefore recognise *their* motives?' asked Chris.

'Because we perceive others' motives as we perceive our own to be,' said Evaluate. 'Your motives are indeed worthy, but it is not until we question and evaluate them that we become absolutely certain of them. Thus your colleagues mistakenly perceive your motives as similar to theirs and, therefore, possible ulterior. And you will assume your colleagues' motives, even Egotist's, to be similar to your own. Tell me, are you able to encapsulate your motives in words right here and now for me?'

'Well,' replied Chris, 'I *feel* them more than I can verbalise them. Though please understand that I am determined to be able to do so now, and very willing to learn how. All I can say to you is that every day I have been becoming more and more frustrated with the level of service and lack of care I see around me. I believe that I have to do something positive to change things but I am not certain how to fulfil my potential to do so.'

'Well answered!' said Evaluate lifting the barrier that separated them. 'Your willingness to exit your current State of Mediocrity is clear to me and, together with your determination, such willingness gains you passage. Here, come through and I will direct you to the next step of your journey.'

Evaluate pointed at the road directly in front of Chris. 'This path before you,' he said, 'is known as the Road of Assessment. You must stay on the road until you come to Accountability's House. Upon your arrival present this evaluation sheet which I have signed and now give to you. Accountability will ensure that you are further prepared for your journey to Service City.'

Chris felt lighter as he walked down the Road of Assessment. He was still aware of his burden, though the firm action he felt he was now taking was clearly alleviating it. Perhaps it was his imagination, yet it seemed that the air here was different. He could breathe deeper than before. He could think. 'This is a strange path,' he said to himself, 'it's not like any other I have been down before. I feel like asking myself questions that I have never asked before, yet in the sure knowledge that the answer will be immediately forthcoming.'

He unrolled the sheet of paper, then looked at Evaluate's signature. As he did so questions seemed to appear on the paper right before his eyes.

'Why do you continue to do only what others think is best for you?'

Almost as soon as he had read the question the answer came into his mind. As it did so, the words appeared beneath the question: *'Because I lack belief in myself.'*

'That's correct,' thought Chris. 'What is this?'

Another question appeared for him to read: *'Why do you feel different when talking to someone you want something from, than when you are talking to someone that you do not want something from?'*

Again the reply appeared before him almost as soon as he had thought of it: *'Because I lack self-confidence in my own innate ability.'*

Chris could not believe his eyes. 'These questions are so hard, yet the answers appear with ease and are so simple.'

'Why do you use a fraction of your potential?' asked another.

'Because I am unaware of my true power,' followed the answer.

'Why do you act as your own worst enemy?'

'Because I don't really like myself.'

'Why are you so easily put off from your course?'

'Because I lack the courage of my convictions.'

'Why do you exist?'

'To fulfil my purpose.'

'What is your purpose?'

'To fulfil my potential.'

There had just been enough room between the words of the last answer and the signature that was at the bottom of the sheet. Chris studied it, drawn by its familiarity. He then recognised it as his own.

As Chris looked up in surprise from the now completed

evaluation sheet, he saw before him a grand, yet welcoming building set back from the road within a walled courtyard. 'This must be Accountability's house,' he said to himself. 'And it would seem that this unusual Road of Assessment has taken me as long as it required me to walk its distance.'

Without pausing, our pilgrim crossed the elegant courtyard, walked up to the large entrance door and rang the bell.

The door was opened a few moments later by Accountability himself who immediately asked Chris where he had travelled from and which way he had come.

Chris related how he had quit the City of Apathy, and the State of Mediocrity, and had travelled via Change Border.

'So you have a completed evaluation sheet for me to consider,' said Accountability expectantly.

'I do indeed,' replied Chris, 'though I was unaware that I had to complete it. Evaluate gave me no such directions, other than signing it and bidding me to give it to you.'

'You will have, no doubt, learned that it is not until we crystallise our thoughts in discussion with others, that we can confirm how we really feel about something, particularly our destiny.'

'Yes,' replied Chris, 'though I am somewhat confused, as there was no one else to discuss my thoughts with other than myself.'

'True,' said Accountability. 'Yet as there can be no better soul to direct you than your own, what better person could you possibly converse with? In important matters of our destiny, there will always be you as you are; you as you think you are; and you as you want others to think that you are. Too often we become so used to relying on the advice of others, that we cease to trust in ourselves. Only through sticking to the path of our own personal assessment will we receive the right answers. Answers that are infinitely more meaningful than those we simply just want to hear.'

> There is the real you; the you that you see yourself as; and the you that you want others to see you as. By using the advice of other people, who see you how you *want* them to see you, you will not get the true advice that is available from within.

With that, Accountability took the evaluation sheet that Chris now offered him and studied it in silence.

'Excellent,' he said, after a few moments. 'Come on in. I'll show you to your room first and later you can meet the others, all of whom are heading towards the Land of Prosperity.'

'Is it a long way?' enquired Chris.

'It is longer for some than others,' replied Accountability, 'which is why your preparation is so important. Is it actually Service City that you want to gain entry?'

'Yes,' said Chris, 'but my burden is so heavy. Are you able to tell me when at last I will be rid of it?'

'Your burden will fall from you of its own accord, when you no longer find solace in it,' answered Accountability.

'But I wasn't aware that I did,' protested Chris.

'People seldom are aware,' said Accountability in reply and led Chris into the house and up to a pleasant room on the first floor. With the room's three aspects, Chris thought he must be in the end wing of the house. One of these windows clearly faced west as Chris could see the beginnings of what would be a dramatic sunset. Another faced north from where he had just come, and overlooked the Road of Assessment. Change Border was nowhere to be seen. 'Strange,' he thought, 'it seems to be much further than I remember.'

'You will probably be more weary than you realise,' continued his host. 'Personal assessment is always exhausting until the mind becomes used to it. Come down to the Library whenever you are ready and join me with the others. Look for the South Wing, you'll find it.'

Lying down on the bed, Chris closed his eyes for what he thought was just a few moments and was surprised to wake up with the room bathed in morning sunlight that poured through the third east-facing window.

After refreshing himself, Chris made his way towards the South Wing.

'It's another beautiful day,' said a voice behind him, who upon catching up with him introduced himself as Enthusiasm.

'How long have you been here?' asked Chris.

'This is my third and last day,' came the reply, 'and the time has absolutely raced by. It always does, of course, when you're enjoying yourself.'

'I only arrived last night,' said Chris, 'but I'm afraid I fell asleep. I hope I didn't miss anything.'

'I wouldn't give it another thought,' said Enthusiasm. 'Accountability says that it is not possible to miss the important lessons of life. And, as we only learn from them when we are ready to receive them, there is little advantage in trying to rush them is there?'

Enthusiasm's light-hearted, positive attitude was infectious and Chris soon found himself laughing as they made their way to the Library together.

The really important lessons in life are never ignored. However, we only learn from them when the time is right for us to do so.

Arriving at the Library Chris was once more welcomed by

Accountability who then proceeded to introduce him to the others that were present.

'I see that you have met with Enthusiasm,' he began. 'No doubt he will have told you that he is leaving us today to continue on his journey. There is much that you can learn from him, so take the opportunity to talk with him before he departs.

'Here is Experience and Youth,' he continued while looking at the two with fond amusement. 'They travel together, though I believe most of their time is spent in disagreement.'

'It's only because he refuses to listen to me,' they both said in unison while pointing at each other.

'It's always the same when they are together,' said Accountability, while guiding Chris across the room, 'both of them always know what to do for the best. Together, however, they make up a strong team, though do not yet realise it. One is more patient than the other, and one is more passionate. Both virtues are complimentary.

'Now, here we have Redundant and Anxious, who arrived last night as you did, though by different roads. And lastly, though by no means least, this is Persistence and Discipline, former students and now colleagues, who drop in from time to time.'

After introductions, Chris turned to Accountability saying, 'Different roads? I thought that there was only the one way to Service City, and that was via Change Border?'

'That's the perfect question with which to commence today's discourse,' he replied and turning to address everyone said, 'The Land of Prosperity occupies its own State of Consciousness. Any change in consciousness must be facilitated by a change in our thinking. But such a change must be in harmony, initially, with what we are used to, culturally. If not, what is being *brought* to us through such change will not be *bought into* by us. We must not seek change for change's sake but for our own sake, to fulfil our potential, so that we can improve our world for the benefit of others. Where numerous religions follow differing paths, for example, all lead from the same spiritual source. Similarly, in seeking the Land of Prosperity, all of your particular paths might at first lead you to different Change Borders. Boundaries that you must each pass through in your own way.'

'Through having to address questions that only we alone can answer?' asked Chris.

> Believe that what you are doing is personally right for you. Only then can you tackle challenges, and changes, with an individual endeavour which will fulfil you *and* enrich the lives of those around you.

'Partly,' replied Accountability. 'The Road of Assessment is certainly the path of many that seek what you seek, though the questions raised may differ. Only you can address your own burden of frustration by first answering your own questions. Redundant here required another route.'

'Yes,' said Redundant, 'I followed the Road of Dilemma, which certainly assisted me in my thinking. For it was not until I walked such a road that I was able to see how my Burden of Predicament would benefit me. I met with Opportunity, who had been going past me, but then who turned and chose to travel with me and brought me here. Opportunity asked questions of me, which prompted me to consider the future differently. That's when I met with Enthusiasm, here.'

'That's right,' volunteered Enthusiasm. 'I had just been enjoying a walk in the courtyard when I noticed Opportunity beckoning towards me.'

'And Enthusiasm brought me into this house and to Accountability,' added Redundant.

'The important thing is that whatever road we decide to take, we ensure that it leads us to taking ownership for such decisions,' said Accountability.

'That sounds all well and good but what if it's just not possible to be on the right road, let alone answer any questions?' put in Anxious.

'By which path did you come to be here then?' enquired Chris.

'Evaluate put me on the Road of Apprehension, then told me I could leave it whenever I wanted. I said it was easy for him to say that, but what if I did and then got lost? But, as I was looking at the road before me, he went and disappeared just leaving me with a blank sheet of paper.'

'Did any questions and answers come to you?' asked Chris.

'Well, in fact, one question did appear, though it gave me no encouragement, answered Anxious. 'It was, "*why are you so fearful about things that never happen?*"'

'And did an answer come to you?' said Chris.

'Well, not really. It was more like a series of alternatives that appeared, though the clearest words read, "Because I enjoy being so".

'Anyway,' continued Anxious, 'just after reading that I met with Self-Pity, who, feeling sorry for me, said he knew somewhere where I may find help, and brought me to the back door of this place. The back door I tell you, just the sort of thing that happens to me!'

'You know that you could have quite easily come round to the front entrance,' said Accountability. 'I believe you already knew that, didn't you?'

'I suppose I did,' Anxious replied, 'and did think about it but, on second thoughts, thought better of it. But I hope you weren't offended,' he added worriedly.

'Perhaps it would be better to have second thoughts first

then,' came the reply. 'Though do not concern yourself, for at this house the front and back doors are one and the same. There can only be one way to enter into taking personal responsibility, which is why you are all here. In preparing yourself to fulfil your potential, there is one prime directive. That is: irrespective of your choices in life, you must always take responsibility for *whatever* happens to you, and always take ownership of that which is important to you, or have promised yourself, or another, to follow through.'

'But what if you choose not to do anything?' asked Youth.

'As even non-choice is a choice by default, you must learn that there is always a choice,' replied Accountability. 'The world recognises no neutral. There is only moving forward or falling back. Our choices or non-choices generate our progress or lack of it.'

> Take responsibility for what happens to you.
> Take ownership of what is important to you.
> Follow your promises, to yourself and others,
> through. This is all part of the preparation for
> fulfilling your potential.

'Surely you don't mean that if I choose not to do anything, I regress?' asked Experience. 'What if such a decision is appropriate? Why, I have learned that it is sometimes far wiser to choose to do nothing, rather than something in a particular situation.'

'Do not mistake non-choice for wrong choice,' replied Accountability. When correct, non-choice will propel you forward, as an incorrect actual choice will force you back. As our choices ultimately shape our destiny, and certainly the level of our success, it is important to learn how to choose correctly.'

'But how is it possible to do that?' asked Anxious.

'By choosing to establish what is important to us, how we

want to live, what we want to do and why we do, and then ensuring that our future choices follow an established format. Success, for example, is commonly thought to be based on good judgement, which in turn is based on experience. And from where is experience gained?'

'Bad judgement,' offered Youth, while poking Experience in the ribs.

'Correct,' said Accountability, 'as I am sure your colleague agrees.'

'It would be wrong of me to say otherwise,' said Experience. 'For, in all honesty, I have probably gained more experience through having to handle my mistakes than anything else. And, certainly, the choices I either make, or choose not to make, these days are infinitely better than they were years ago, though I cannot admit to them being within an established framework. But then that is why I am here.'

'By which road then did you come to be here?' asked Chris.

'By the Road of Futility,' replied Experience, 'where I learned that a wealth of knowledge is useless without purposeful goals to harness and direct it.'

Without purposeful goals to direct it, a wealth of knowledge has little value.

'That was my road too, though the questions that came to me were not the same as yours, were they?' said Youth looking at Experience. 'I discovered that unless I take the time to know what I really want to do in my life, I will never be able to fulfil my true potential.'

'Certainly, you must enjoy, even love, what you do in life to make the most of your potential,' cut in Enthusiasm. 'It's almost as though really enjoying something is a clear sign to you of your reason for being.'

'Let's get real here,' said Anxious. 'You can't always do what you *enjoy* doing. Sometimes, in fact most of the time, I don't enjoy what I do, but I do it because I have to. How else could I afford to live?'

'When people choose, usually through non-choice, *not* to do what they really want, they will complain about what they *have* to do, even though they do not know what they would *rather* do,' said Accountability. 'If only they could stop to think about what they truly enjoy doing and work towards it.'

'People will unconsciously take more time trying to get out of something, or spend more energy getting around something, than simply just getting on with it,' said Discipline. 'If they were simply to put some energy and enthusiasm into the task, they would get more out of it and so would their customer.'

'Yes!' said Chris. 'I'm sure that's exactly what happens when people serve others. So many of us are ingenious in devising ways of getting out of what we are actually working towards when this doesn't help anyone. Whenever you walk up to a service counter, whether you want to hire a car, check into a flight desk, or even announce your arrival for a dental appointment, people seem determined to make you wait before acknowledging you. Even if it's only for a few seconds, you feel as if what you have to say is not important, because they are not interested in talking to you and it's as if they are doing you a huge favour when they finally do.'

'It's certainly a good feeling when they *do* acknowledge you in a way that shows they are pleased to see you, even if they are attending to someone else,' said Enthusiasm. 'Like that continental courtesy of welcoming a customer as soon as they come through the shop door. Just being acknowledged in this way means so much.'

At any time in your life you are either in
control, or being controlled. Insecure people
feel stronger when controlling others. It is
only a temporary strength because it is based
on uncertainty.

'Whenever people are uncertain about what they really want
to do, they will feel insecure,' said Accountability. 'Whenever
people harbour insecurities, whatever they are and for whatever
reason, they will unconsciously compensate by seeking control
over others. Controlling another, even just keeping them waiting
for a split second, restores a sense of power within an individual.
Though, in reality, this power is short-lived and soon relin-
quished, because it is a false sense of security.' Accountability
paused to allow his words to be taken in.

'To serve another well,' he continued, 'is therefore perceived
as a weakness, instead of the strength that it really is. I said earlier
that the Land of Prosperity was a State of Consciousness that
required a different level of thinking. A level that recognises
that giving service is a strength; that understands the importance
of continuous personal and professional development in order
to fulfil potential; and that acknowledges the importance of
aligning what we do with what we are within a specific
framework of mission, goals, values and personal ethos.

'The future of worthwhile success is exemplified in Service
City. Those of you who are determined to enter it will discover
this for yourself and enjoy rewards that are abundantly available
and beyond your expectations. There you will discover that
words are meaningless in themselves. For it is people's actions
that have meaning, actions that speak volumes. In the course of
your journey there you will, however, encounter many places
where it is considered that words are sufficient in themselves.
Some proclaim the words so much that they end up resting solely

on them for future growth and relying on them for establishing a reputation or position in the marketplace. People, in fact, know not what they do.'

'You are so right,' agreed Chris. 'Every day I work with people who only focus on what they can say to market products in the most exciting way. The meaning is lost in the method. Their aim is merely to move products as quickly as possible and the fact that what they are saying about these products is not strictly true seems to be of little interest to them. It's "all part of the job" as far as they are concerned!'

> Being responsible for actions requires taking ownership of your decisions and being accountable for following them.

'Your time here is to prepare you for seeing through these places that rely on strong, though meaningless words. Those of you who choose to learn from your impending journey will be rewarded by gaining entry into Service City. But remember, though many would like to live there, profit and prosper, only the most committed, and who have the right motives, will be able to do so.

'On the way here you all questioned yourself as to your motives for the journey you are embarking upon. At this point only *you* will know what work you have to do in that area, because only you will understand your own motives and be able to make your own decisions based on those motives. We have today shared with each other the importance of recognising our power of choice. Always remember that, irrespective of your circumstances and conditions, you are where you are *because* of your previous choices or non-choices. It follows, therefore, that you can be whatever you want to be, do whatever you want to do and have whatever you want to have when you make a definite choice to take action. This action will involve accepting full personal responsibility for whatever happens in your life. However hard it is for you to accept this, it is vital that you still do so. You, and only you, are responsible for you.

> First make the choice to take a particular course of action, then take full responsibility for what happens as a result. Now you can really be the person you want to be, do what you deeply want to do, and have what you truly want to have.

'Following this truth, you must always choose to take ownership of your decisions and become accountable for following whatever they are through.' Accountability turned towards where Discipline and Persistence were seated and asked, 'Perhaps you would tell us of the roads you came by?'

'I have always chosen to take the same road whenever I visit here,' began Discipline. 'I know it well and it serves me well, and the more that I continue to travel it, the faster I seem able to move. Straight though well worn, as it is often used for exercise, it is named the Road of Preparation.'

'It sounds a good road,' said Chris, 'but tell me, do the same questions appear to you each time you walk such a path?'

'They are similar yet seem to become more testing each time,' replied Discipline, 'and though the answers differ slightly, they become perhaps more accurate each time. I remember one of the first questions asked was, *Why do you keep putting things off?* To which the answer came: *Because they are not important.*

'Then, another time, the question asked, *Why do you keep putting important things off?* This time the answer was: *Because they are important.* A third time the question asked, *Why do you leave what is so important for you to do until the last minute?* And the answer was: *Because I am lazy.*'

'Surely that can't be right,' said Chris. 'You appear to be so, well, *orderly*, if you understand me.'

'Thank you, but I wasn't always so,' replied Discipline. 'But let me tell you that travelling the Road of Preparation taught me that laziness comes upon us when we lack motivation for what we want to achieve. Having a goal is not as important as knowing *why* you want to achieve it. When you have many reasons for *why* you actually want to be, do or have something, the *preparation* is important to ensure their fulfilment becomes something you look forward to.'

> Lack of reasons is why people do not achieve what they are capable of in life, not lack of goals.

'I agree,' said Persistence. 'Most people do not achieve what they are capable of in life because of *lack of goals*, but because of *lack of reasons* to achieve their goals. Travelling the Road of Tenacity as I did taught me the importance of measuring the belief in oneself. A belief that can really only be proved when it becomes clear that you will stick to doing something regardless of the obstacles that are in the way of its achievement.'

'That may be true, but most people lack goals, let alone reasons to have them,' said Anxious.

'A person must always have goals, for if they don't know where they are going, how will they recognise it when they get there?' replied Persistence. 'That is why so many people feel lost even when they are in familiar surroundings. The difficulty is that people generally only have goals for what they want to have.'

'And you cannot have before you do, nor do before you can be,' said Discipline.

'Absolutely, and you can only be tenacious in following through your goals, if they excite you,' added Persistence.

'For such excitement is a measure in how much you want to achieve them,' put in Enthusiasm.

'Where I used to work, we were told to make goals but, to be honest, none of them really *excited* me,' said Redundant.

'That's because they were not goals that had meaning to you,' said Accountability. 'And the danger is that when we have no belief in what we are about, it is reflected in our attitude and behaviour towards others. You might say that we become *demeaning* towards others, particularly if we have to serve them as part of the accomplishment of such goals.'

People feel wrongly that others think they are demeaning themselves through the acts of giving good service. This makes them behave in a demeaning manner to customers to try and redress the balance.

'I suppose I did feel a little like that, but I did enjoy my work. It's what I knew and I was good at it. Though seldom was much recognition forthcoming,' said Redundant. 'I was part of a strategy team for my former employer, All Tech-no-Com. Our team's role was to formulate innovative ways to get our customers to stay with us, rather than leave and join one of our many competitors. This was quite challenging because in our industry a product could be out of date almost as soon as it was available.

'In deciding to create a particular strategy, unless we were able to get it adopted quickly and prove that it was generating growth, it would lose its impetus and our work would be in vain. Because of this, not as much preparation was carried out as perhaps should have been. And we were seldom able to follow things through, because someone in another department would veto it. Would you believe that as many as five signatures from various senior managers were required before something could be agreed to? Anyway, and to make matters worse, one of the signatories would ratify strategy only on the basis of how it affected him. His name was Credit-Seek and I am sure that he was responsible for many colleagues and myself being considered as an unnecessary overhead.'

'He was responsible?' said Accountability. 'Remember that regardless of whatever happens we must take responsibility.'

'But why should I,' protested Redundant, 'if it wasn't my fault?'

'Simply because by doing so you let go of the emotional baggage the experience has created,' answered Accountability. 'And because blaming others, which is spawned from not taking personal responsibility ourselves, looks backward; whereas solution, derived from taking responsibility, looks only forward. *And* you have recently learned that when you look forward, opportunity appears, doesn't it?'

> Blame looks backward. Solution looks only
> forward. Missed opportunities are in the past.
> Look forward and opportunities appear.

'It does seem that the higher some people go in a firm the more they become concerned about securing what they have already achieved,' said Persistence. 'It's almost as if their focus changes from aspiring to what they want, to one of keeping what they have achieved.'

'Well, Credit-Seek was certainly one of those,' said Redundant. 'It was as if he used all the experience that he had gained over the years to recognise what would bring benefit to him. I remember that there was an analytical report that had been produced for years. It took several people weeks to prepare and it was never read. It was just one of those things that had always been done. Our team suggested that it was no longer necessary and that there could be a better use of resources. Well, even though Credit-Seek admitted to never having read it himself, he was concerned that he might be blamed for stopping it by someone who did read it, so he wouldn't ratify the idea. But one of our team mistakenly assumed that he had agreed to the suggestion and the report was stopped. A long time afterwards it was noticed that the research team, who had in the past prepared the report, was getting better results. When asked how this was, they said that as they no longer had to waste time putting together long reports they could get on with more important work. Well, no prizes for guessing who took advantage of this. Sure enough, Credit-Seek made out that it had been his idea all along.'

'That must have been demoralising for your team?' said Chris.

'It certainly was. When we got something wrong, everyone heard about it and when we got it right, we received no praise. Mind you, the service team had a worse deal. Because All Tech-no-Com insisted on zero defects as a policy they set up a specific rapid response team to ensure that this could be brought about. Their job was to use their technology to know about an occurring fault even *before* the customer. They were so successful that they were never mentioned, until Finance saw what they were spending, couldn't believe how much it was and immediately reduced their budget. Shortly afterwards the service team was taken to task for having allowed defects and therefore customer complaints to increase.'

'But surely your company must have recognised that the service team's budget had been solely responsible for reduced customer complaints?' asked Chris.

'Not really,' replied Redundant, 'for they had just invested in a Customer Complaints Department who had to be busy to justify its existence. Finance decided that it was pointless having two expensive units, so one of them had to be cut. It was felt that as Customer Complaints interfaced directly with the customer, whereas the Service Team did not, they were better positioned to mollify the customer and maintain customer loyalty.'

'What do you mean by interfaced?' asked Accountability.

'To talk to them,' volunteered Youth.

'Then why not say that?' said Experience.

'Because talking to them might be by computer or electronic voice mail,' said Youth.

'But how is it possible to build loyalty through this inter-facing?' said Accountability. 'Surely loyalty is brought about through building relationships, which involves both talk and action?'

During the course of the next three days, Chris took the opportunity to spend time with each of Accountability's houseguests.

'I really don't see how anything can be achieved without your involvement,' he said to Enthusiasm, prior to the latter's departure on the first day. 'Couldn't you stay just a little longer, for there is so much more I want to ask you?'

'Don't worry,' Enthusiasm replied. 'The rate at which you are working on yourself it will not be long before you run into your own inspiration. And, for the sake of your successful progress, let me tell you that it is a far better thing to acquire your own strength than simply borrow strength from another. For, in doing the latter, that which we have the ability to do well and really excel at can be lost to us.'

It is more powerful and permanent to gain strength through your own efforts and experiences than to borrow it from other people.

'But how can we be sure that we have such strength and abilities?' Chris asked. 'Surely some people are simply more gifted than others are? After all, we can't all be geniuses.'

'Why not?' answered Enthusiasm. 'Of course we can, because we already are. It's simply that most people have been conditioned to believe that they are ordinary, instead of the *extra*ordinary beings that they really are. Those who are able to express the real extra-ordinary self are simply acting in harmony, either consciously or unconsciously, with their true potential. Others, who are occupied with what they think they should be *doing*, never find the time to follow their hearts' desire for *being* what they are intended to be. Yet the fact is we are human beings, not human doings.

'Desire is the starting point of all achievement. You would not have the desire unless you had the ability to achieve whatever it was in the first place. But the real determining factor is how strong the desire is. For, without doubt, many desires may be ignited but almost all are allowed to fizzle out. Yet, understand that only a deep burning desire will allow you to tap into the rich resources of your own incredible, though dormant, potential.'

'But it's not good to always desire something is it?' asked Chris.

'Why ever not? It's the most natural emotion in the world. The desire to survive is shared by every living creature. The desire to grow and fulfil its potential is the very element of Nature itself. Does a tree grow to half its height? No, it grows as tall as it possibly can. Desire is a positive and vital part of being human, though, like many powerful factors, its power can be abused and mistakenly applied.'

'How exactly?' asked Chris. 'I have to admit that whenever

I've had the desire to do something that I believe will improve my life, I've always felt guilty for not just being satisfied with what I already have.'

'It isn't good to be *dis*satisfied, but this is not the same as being *un*satisfied,' replied Enthusiasm. 'Can a person really be satisfied if they know that they are using just a small portion of their abilities? Certainly not, and if they continue in this way, that lack of challenge will cause atrophy. That is the very weakening of their abilities. The result is that people will still have desires, but now emotional energy is attached to the outcome, instead of being used to drive the ability that feeds the desire.

'Now, although people choose to believe that they have control over their outcomes, they do not. They only have control over their ability to drive the process. With emotional energy attached to the importance of the outcome, instead of the very process to bring it about, few desires are fulfilled. Consequently, people do not feel good, and when they do not feel good they blame the desire for having put themselves in that state. Hence the belief that desires are not good.'

> Don't try to control end results because of
> the emotions you have attached to them.
> Instead concentrate only on the process that
> will increase your potential to realise your
> desires, and decrease your frustrations.

'And what is then felt is a sense of frustration, I suppose,' said Chris.

'Whenever desires are not forthcoming you will feel this. But as you follow the path that has meaning to you, you will start to feel the excitement of what you are about begin to grow within you. Keep it alive, recognising it as the indication of what you are already capable of achieving and, as I discovered for myself on the Road of Devotion, your growing enthusiasm will diminish your current burden.'

'I was wondering by what road you came to be here,' said Chris.

'It was the perfect road for me,' said Enthusiasm. 'For it was on such a path that I learned to devote myself to what was important to me. Prior to this there were times when my abilities were used in such a way that gave me no satisfaction at all. Indeed, all I got for my efforts was a growing burden of dismay. Now, of course, my eagerness for what I am doing knows no bounds and the wonderful thing is that the more I share it with others, the more I seem to have.'

'Well, it is certainly contagious,' laughed Chris. 'I can feel it growing in me.'

'Of course!' said Enthusiasm, as he got up to depart. 'For it is the nature of such a thing only to grow. And you must allow it to continue to do so as it is the very *armour* inside you that will protect you in those battles that lie ahead of you. But here, allow me to give you these Mettle Gauntlets from my own hands. They have served me well and will help you to overcome such battles. Now I must go. Goodbye!'

Chris looked at the Mettle Gauntlets before him for a moment in bewilderment. 'Wait,' he shouted after Enthusiasm, 'what battles?'

'The ones you seek out yourself, of course,' shouted back Enthusiasm. 'But remember that the only things we never lose are the things we give away.'

Harnessing the energies of all, for the benefit of all requires the ability to communicate vision.

'Coming through the State of Chaos on my way here was

not easy,' said Discipline, 'but the key is not to quarrel, or fall out, with anyone there. No, rather it is to marshal all of Chaos. For when it is organised around a unified purpose, a lot of creativity is forthcoming.'

'I would not have thought that good would come from being in such a State,' said Chris, who had begun his conversation with Discipline by asking where he was from.

'Few people living outside such a State do, and even those people who choose to live there seldom accept that such a thing is possible. None the less, it would seem that the best disciplines come out of such an environment. Why, even out of the chaos of an exploding void came the creation of a Universe that is able to maintain itself in perfect balance. Even your enormous City of Apathy, if seen from way above, would appear as an ant hill. Everyone rushing hither, and thither, yet all with something to do.'

'But nowhere in particular to go,' put in Chris.

'To them they have, because that is all they know and people are comfortable doing what they know.'

'How do you go about marshalling chaos for creativity, as you say, and why would the outcome create good attributes of discipline?' enquired Chris.

'I didn't say that one led to the other,' replied Discipline, 'indeed both are independent. Though they may emanate from the same environment, which is conducive for them, they follow different paths. To marshal chaos requires the ability to communicate the vision of a unified and common purpose that will harness the energies of all, for the benefit of all. Irrespective of the vision, receptivity for what its achievement will deliver must be created. When people believe in a vision, the potential that is released and the enormous energy that is focused because people *want* to work, rather than have to, for a common purpose is immeasurable. If you are successful in entering Service City

61

you will learn more on this subject, but first you must cultivate certain attributes to be able to get there.'

'I am willing to learn whatever is necessary,' volunteered Chris.

'Good,' said Discipline. 'One of the hardest obstacles you will come across can become insurmountable, even though it is passable. Yet it is this obstacle that you *must* overcome.'

'What on earth is it and do I *have* to come across it?' pleaded Chris. 'Surely there must be an alternative path.'

'There is, but people rarely find it. It's as if they attract the obstacle, which is like a terrible monster, whatever way they go. If it meets you, this hideous creature, sometimes referred to as the destroyer of dreams, will viciously attack you. Going under the name of Securi-I-tas, it has crossed the path of many unsuspecting pilgrims journeying towards the Land of Prosperity.'

'How can I protect myself against such a monster?' cried Chris.

'With the armour that Enthusiasm has already advised you carry within you, his own Mettle Gauntlets that he has given to you and with the Shield of Sequence that I myself shall give you. With this you will be able to take one sure step at a time and not give way to the monster's attack.'

'And with the Sword of Steadfastness that I am able to offer, you will be able to get past it and cut your way through,' said Persistence who now joined them.

'But remember to use both the shield and the sword at the same time,' said Discipline, 'as sequential steadfastness is an important key to success in your journey.'

'And the more that you continue on your chosen path in the face of all your obstacles, the more belief and confidence grows in you,' added Persistence.

'Yes, I recall one pilgrim, Analysis, who was religious about the path he was taking,' said Discipline. 'His self-control was clear for all to see, yet he lacked the tenacity to follow things through. No sooner would he come upon an obstacle than he would back off and take another path. He was the most organised and prepared of travellers, but without steadfastness his sequential progress caused him to go round in circles.'

'Did he get where he was going in the end, though?' asked Chris.

'Well, the last I heard of him was that he was trying to find a way across the Chasm of Professional Complacency, just outside Service City.'

'With another traveller,' put in Persistence, 'who I recall excelled at perseverance, but lacked self-government, the result was that he was never prepared to move forward.'

'That's right,' added Discipline, 'his name was Paralysis. And now the two of them unwittingly cause doubts in the minds of other travellers who are nearing the end of their journey.'

'But you would have thought that together they could have helped each other,' said Chris.

'I'm afraid that's not always the case, especially when both the impediments hold the most influence,' answered Discipline. 'The result is that the team of Analysis-Paralysis now perceive their duty as one of confronting and questioning pilgrims to see if they should really continue forward or turn back.'

To move forward and successfully overcome challenges you need to use all your strengths and abilities.

As it was nearing the time that he must depart, Chris went to see Accountability. His host was in conversation with Anxious and Redundant.

'Our self-concept is effectively our command centre,' said

Accountability. 'And whatever we believe about ourselves becomes true, as we act in a manner which is consistent with those beliefs. There are three parts to our command; our self-ideal, or the person we would most like to be; our self-image, or the person we think ourselves to be; and our self-esteem, or how much we feel we like the person that we are.'

'I still don't see how learning to like ourselves more puts us on the road to improvement,' said Anxious. 'What will people think of us if they find out we are wanting to like ourselves more?'

'Well, as I understand it,' said Redundant, 'if we don't really like ourselves 100 per cent, we're not going to really believe in ourselves. And if self-confidence must be acquired to reach our self-ideal, then I for one am going to learn to like myself more. Mind you, it's going to be hard because I never really valued myself perhaps as much as I should have.'

'A person's self-worth receives many knocks,' offered Accountability, 'even by well meaning people. But be assured that it, and your esteem, will grow in direct proportion to how much you like and respect yourself. For you must respect yourself. Indeed your self-respect is the greatest treasure you possess, so you must never give it away by being embarrassed for who you are, or what you do.'

> Your self-worth and self-esteem will grow only
> if you like yourself, and have respect for
> yourself. Don't give away your self-respect as
> it is very precious.

'I have learned during these last few intensive days,' put in Chris, 'that the development of a wholesome self-respect and positive self-image are closely related to the recognition of the unlimited potential that exists in each of us.'

'Quite right,' said Accountability beaming, 'and we must never short-circuit our chances of releasing such potential by having a poor self-image. One that insists on us placing a ceiling on all of our genuinely attainable aspirations.'

'So come on,' said Redundant to Anxious, 'let's go and continue our studies on this one. There's no way I want to limit what I want to do and where I want to go, now that I have met with Opportunity!'

As Accountability watched the two leave the room he said, 'Well Chris, your stay here is at an end and I am sure that you are eager to continue on your way.'

'I am indeed, ready or not,' answered Chris.

'You are as ready as you will ever be, for it is only through following your destiny that you prepare yourself for it,' said Accountability.

'I am still somewhat weighed down with my burden of frustration though and I am concerned about forthcoming obstacles, though hopefully I won't meet with them,' said Chris. 'But I feel that my resolve is firm and I will meet what I must.'

'Experience will tell you that for every battle won or lost, you will emerge stronger, so long as you look for the inherent lesson of each battle,' said Accountability. 'If you ask Youth, he will tell you that to live and not to risk, is not to be born. Both are right, as usual of course, and in truth, timber becomes stronger through rough weather. You may feel your resolve is firm, but it will not be until it is tested on the road that you will see if it remains firm. But I have a gift for you, to go with the gifts my colleagues have given you. Here is a Helmet of Conscience, which will protect you from any monster that is intent on leading you to doubt either your resolve or responsibility.'

'You believe that I will have to battle with Securi-I-tas, then?'

'I hope not, but it is better that we enter upon the unknown with as much preparation as we are able to draw upon. Remember to always keep your mind on what you want, why you seek it and why it caused you to leave the State of Mediocrity. Never allow yourself to be persuaded to dwell on what you don't want because you may discover, as many others have done to their distress, that you unconsciously gravitate towards it.'

'Now,' said Accountability, opening the large entrance door and pointing towards the gates, 'allow me to set you in the right direction, for there is one other that you must meet with. There is no need to go through the gates you entered by. Once we have understood the importance of taking ownership for what happens to us in our lives, there can be no going back to how we were. When you cross this courtyard, you will now be able to see an opening in the side of the wall.'

'Yet, when I arrived I marvelled at how self-contained the courtyard appeared to be,' said Chris.

'Of course, for it appeared as you imagined it to be. After you pass through the opening in the wall, you will hear a waterfall. Follow the sound and you will come upon a gazebo at the head of a lake. Upon entering you will see someone who is waiting there to speak to you.'

'But who is it?' enquired Chris with curiosity.

'You'll see,' answered Accountability. 'Now, good luck and be careful you don't miss the gazebo. With the sun reflecting off the lake, as it does, others have sadly passed by without noticing it.'

To Be a Pilgrim ...

- Follow your chosen path to be in the right place at the right time
- Consciously evaluate your motives on a regular basis
- Crystallise your thoughts in writing
- Take ownership of your dreams and watch them come true
- Know that *deeds*, not words, have meaning so your actions speak volumes
- Accept that you are where you are because of previous choices or non-choices
- Acquire your own strength rather than borrow that of another
- Consider self-respect as your greatest treasure never to be buried or lost

Chapter Three

Climbing the Hill of Reluctance

As soon as Chris passed through the opening in the courtyard, he heard the sound of falling water. Following it, he soon came upon a bubbling brook where the water persistently bounced from stone to stone, earnestly pursuing the deep course that it had succeeded in carving.

'Who would have thought that such a small stream could make such a mark?' thought Chris as he tracked it downstream to where he was certain he could make out the familiar sound of a waterfall. Reaching the point where the water threw itself down to the pool of water below, he was surprised at the size of the lake that flowed beneath. 'And who would have thought that it could feed such a large lake.'

The light was reflecting so brightly off the water that his vision was momentarily impeded. But he was just able to make out a small bower to the side of the lake. 'That must be the gazebo,' he said out loud to himself and walked towards it.

'Ah,' said Inspiration to Chris as the latter entered, 'come in. I've been expecting you.'

'How could you have been expecting me?' asked Chris.

'I am always expecting someone to pass by,' Inspiration replied. 'No doubt you have just departed Accountability's house? Was the time you spent there of use to you?'

'Most definitely,' answered Chris. 'For I began to understand the importance that personal development holds with regard to entering Service City.'

'Good, so you have come here to develop your own charter then?'

'Have I?' replied Chris with uncertainty. 'I'm actually passing through here because Accountability advised me that there was another I must meet.'

'And you chose to follow his advice, chose to look out for this retreat and chose to enter,' said Inspiration.

'Well, yes, I suppose I did.'

'Good because, having understood the importance of evaluating yourself, personal choice in your life and taking ownership for what you do, the time has come to create your own charter for what you stand for.'

'My own charter?' repeated Chris.

'Absolutely,' said Inspiration. 'A charter that encapsulates your reason for being. A guiding statement that serves as a reminder to align what you do with what you are. You will not be able to enter Service City without having your own charter. Why, it is *the* motive certificate that is essential to being able to give Enlightened Service. The incredible rewards that will be forthcoming to you in Service City are not yours without it. I see that you already have protection against negative influences and weapons to overcome obstacles, but without a standard to bear, what will inspire you to fight for what you believe in?'

> Understand how important it is to evaluate yourself, to make personal choices and take ownership of what you do, and it will be the right time to set down what you stand for in your own charter.

'I had not thought of it like that,' said Chris.

'Well you must!' said Inspiration. 'Because the people who choose to live in Service City *all* know what they *stand* for. They are committed to setting *the* services standard that all other cities will one day aspire to. The King there only accepts the very best and is only interested in those people who give their best *because* they *want* to.'

'Then I want to bear such a standard,' said Chris. 'What must I do?'

'Look at this lake in front of us,' began Inspiration. 'It owes its size, content, depth and strength to this sparkling stream that flows into it. See how small the stream is compared to the lake, yet it provides a constant supply of water. It is the lake's conduit for life. The stream itself knows its destination as soon as it springs from its source. In its determination, it seeks the path of the least resistance, yet is not put off its course by the obstacles it meets. It does not look to force its way by pushing and shoving, rather it overcomes all by its very commitment to get where it's going. See how it seems to joyfully bounce from stone to stone harnessing each obstacle as allies to carve its path. And look at the path it has marked out, its own statement for all to know what it is about. This stream knows the importance of turning a sense of longing into a sense of belonging. It carries no frustration; it simply carries an acknowledgement for its very existence, its *raison d'être*.

'Now,' continued Inspiration, 'what do you do and is there a *raison d'être* where you work?'

'I am the sales and marketing director at Communication Limited in the City of Apathy,' replied Chris. 'A mission statement does exist; though I am not sure whether it encapsulates what we are about, like a *raison d'être* as you say.'

'Did everybody in the company have a part in developing its meaning?' asked Inspiration.

71

'Not at all,' answered Chris, 'though I believe *most* people were not really concerned.'

'Perhaps because they considered it as just another programme of the month?' enquired Inspiration.

'Well, yes, I suppose some people have made comments to that effect,' said Chris.

'And the people who were involved in producing it, did they already have personal mission statements?'

'Not that I know of, although I wasn't involved in it too much anyway.'

'Would you say that a harmonious atmosphere existed? One that was conducive to a sense of belonging?'

Chris thought of his own sense of longing and of the duplicitous 'that's-not-your-job' and 'didn't-you-know' environment that was the basis of Communication Limited. 'I believe that developing and communicating our mission to everyone was supposed to create such an atmosphere, but it certainly hasn't been successful. Everyone just ignores it and gets on with what they have to do. In fact, our company's culture is not good, we're a communication company yet we don't seem able to communicate between ourselves, let alone our customers.'

'A legal document may form a company,' said Inspiration. 'But it can only be people that can ever make it come alive. And it is how they think and feel about what they do that will generate the culture of work there. Whenever people are not interested in being part of something, whatever they are part of will not hold meaning in their life. Even though their involvement may well develop greater commitment, it will be short-lived unless they understand and acknowledge what developing a charter involves; and recognise and accept the importance of actually going through the process of developing one for themselves.'

Developing a personal mission enables you to see if you want to align what is important to you with what you actually do.

'It does seem to make sense for individuals to have their own mission statement, or charter,' said Chris. 'It's true that the mission of Communication Limited has not been bought into because people have not been part of the process, so perhaps do not warm to what it stands for. But surely they'd need some guidance otherwise everybody would do their own thing?'

'What's important in developing a personal mission is that in doing so they will be able to see clearly for themselves if they want to align what is *important to them* with what they *actually do*. Some people will acknowledge to themselves that they have been difficult and resistant to new ideas, change and service simply because they had not recognised that it was important to them. In recognising that what they are doing is very much a part of something, a cause, rather than just a job, they view their work as a different vehicle than they had previously thought. A vehicle worth being part of, and one that will take them to where they want to go.

'Others will choose to leave the vehicle, recognising that it is not as important to them as doing something else and are therefore not giving to it as much as they should. Such action is good for both the company and the individual, for who wants to work with another just because it is something to do and pays the bills?

'The end result is that everyone shares a unified purpose. Clearly, the leaders who are responsible for driving the business and whose prime function is to communicate the vision of where it is going and why, have a duty to provide guidance. But they can only achieve this through their own example. They, above all, must go through the process of knowing what they stand for. If not, how can it be possible to develop something that reflects what everyone involved in a business stands for?'

'Intuition told me that it is not possible to complain about the state of the street, unless first your own house is in order,' said Chris.

'And as always, my good friend is right,' said Inspiration. 'That principle is immutable, though rarely acknowledged. But come, *you* have already done the groundwork to put your house in order. Are you ready to know what you stand for? To embrace those values and principles that will guide your every decision?'

'Yes,' said Chris, 'I am inspired to do so, though I am not certain how to put my feelings into words.'

'Go for it anyway. Feel what you feel and just let the words flow. What gives you your burden of frustration?'

'Not being able to do what I know I am capable of.'

'Which is?'

'Delivering what I fully believe in, selling what I believe in, marketing what I believe in, being what I believe in.'

'Which is?'

'Making a difference in the lives of others and thereby continually improving my own.'

'Following the principle that the best way to learn is to teach?' offered Inspiration.

'Yes, because the best way to serve yourself is to serve others,' said Chris, feeling the words coming from his heart and hearing them begin to flow from his lips.

'So?'

'I stand for learning about myself through teaching good service.

'I stand for treating everyone equally in the same way that I would like to be treated irrespective of title, rank, background, education, colour, sex, or creed.

'I stand for treating the person *behind* the desk in the same way as the person *in front of* the desk.

'I stand for treating the person in front of the desk as if he, or she, were my customer for life, even if they are not.

'I stand for continually seeking ways to always surprise the people that I serve, by going the extra mile.

'I stand for *people* before *products*, *service* before *selling* and *relationships* before *marketing*.

'I stand for doing the right thing, before doing things right, even if it means *losing* a sale. Because I stand for *delivering* what my customer wants, before *selling* them what I want.

'Above all, I stand for *character* before *personality* and being internally motivated rather than externally influenced.'

Chris paused, took a deep breath and said. '*I stand to deliver.*'

'Excellent!' said Inspiration. 'The simplest statements are always the best to remind us of what we stand for, particularly when doubts cause us to question what we are about.'

'Something feels different,' said Chris. 'It's as though something has been lifted from me.'

'Perhaps it has,' suggested Inspiration.

'My burden!' cried out Chris. 'My burden of frustration has been taken away from me! It's gone, at last it's gone!'

'Of course!' said Inspiration. 'Every burden disappears when we address why we have it in the first place.'

'I feel so much lighter, more confident, more certain of my direction!' said Chris, excitedly.

'Good, and just at the right time too. You are now ready to continue your journey towards the Land of Prosperity and Service City itself,' said Inspiration.

Chris could hardly contain his gratitude. 'I just can't thank you enough,' he said. 'You have no idea what shedding my burden means to me! I feel so good!'

'It is true that having such a burden would be difficult for me to imagine,' replied Inspiration. 'I very much appreciate your thanks, though I am just as grateful that you chose to pass by this way and talk with me. Few take the time to do so, often relying on the false belief that their burdens are something they have to learn to live with. You can imagine how quiet it can be here with few pilgrims such as yourself.'

If you address the reasons why you feel weighed down by a particular problem or worry you will find it diminishes.

'Perhaps most start with good intentions but get distracted from their path,' said Chris thinking of how he was almost lost in the Wilderness of Conformity.

'Perhaps,' repeated Inspiration. 'But look, take this Charter, which I give to you now, and keep it safe,' said Inspiration. 'It is a Certificate of Motive that will continue to become more meaningful as you keep your objective in mind. Don't lose it, for you will want to show it to the gatekeepers at Service City. Take the path beyond the lake that leads upwards, towards that large hill you can see in the distance. That is the Hill of Reluctance and you must follow the path that leads to the very top. It is by far the best route to Integrity House where you will be able to rest. Away now and good luck!'

With much lighter steps our pilgrim followed the path beyond the lake towards the Hill of Reluctance. Approaching it he saw that the path split into three ways. Two were going around the Hill and one continued upwards. There were two people at the junction.

'Ah, a fellow traveller,' said Quick-Fix, as one of the two

was named. 'Someone who can share his story while we walk will pass the time quicker.'

'Well, it would be good to wile away a couple of hours,' said Trivia, to his companion and turning towards Chris added, 'Hi, you're just in time to join us.'

'Good,' said Chris, and laughingly added, 'I would like that, though this Hill looks steeper than it did at a distance. We might not have enough breath to talk as well, eh?'

'You're not considering taking that route are you?' said Quick-Fix. 'Taking this side road will get us to our destination much faster.'

'Well, I'm not sure where you two are heading, but my next destination is Integrity House, which I understand, lies this way,' said Chris pointing at the road which led up.

'That won't get you anywhere in a hurry,' scoffed Quick-Fix. 'No, this side road is much easier and will still get us there. I've heard of Integrity House, it's on the road to the Ground of Good Fortune, which is where we're bound for anyway. So, if you come with us, I'm sure that we will pass by the place.'

'Our way is far more enjoyable,' added Trivia. 'There are lots of little things to see on the way, which are great for occupying the mind while walking and talking.'

'Much as I appreciate your kind offer of company and conversation, I will follow the path ahead of me,' said Chris. 'Yes, it is steep, but I take the view that I will be rewarded for my efforts.'

'I would strongly warn you about taking such a road for it would be a bad choice,' argued Quick-Fix. 'Let me tell you that we actually started to go that way, but the path is hardly worn and looked as if it led nowhere.'

'And it looked boring, as well as tiring,' added Trivia. 'Come on, join us, the more the merrier I always say.'

'No,' said Chris, surprised at how firm he sounded. 'This path is for me, onwards and up, I say.'

'Well more fool you!' retorted Quick-Fix. 'You don't know *what* you're missing out on,' and turning to his companion added, 'come on, we've wasted enough time as it is. Let's go!'

Chris took the opportunity to rest a short time, before continuing, and watched the two as they left. After a few minutes Chris saw Trivia stop and beckon to Quick-Fix and then point at something in the distance. A few minutes after that Trivia stopped again and once more beckoned his companion. This happened a couple more times until it appeared to Chris that the two were exchanging heated words. Quick-Fix then turned and walked back to the junction.

'So, you've decided to join me after all,' said Chris when they were in earshot of each other.

'There's no way I'm going up that Hill,' replied Quick-Fix breathlessly. 'No, I'm just taking this other side road, which will be just as quick I'm sure. And I'll be much faster than being bogged down with Trivia over there! I can't imagine for one moment how he finds so much time to waste in trying to get where he's going. That's if he knows where he's going, as I do.' Soon both Trivia and Quick-Fix had disappeared from view as they set off on their respective routes, and Chris started up the hill road.

'I'm sure this path is becoming steeper,' thought Chris after he had been climbing for what seemed ages. 'This is hard work and I am only about halfway up.'

'At least you stopped at the best place to rest,' said a voice, 'just look at the view.'

'And how do you know that it's the best place?' asked Chris pleasantly.

'Because, I have been here for some time. My name's Habit

and I call this idyllic place my comfort zone. Here, come and take a break for a while, you've earned it!'

'Thanks,' said Chris, while introducing himself and choosing a spot to sit down. 'You're right, it seems a good place to rest.'

'And a great view to enjoy as well, eh?' said Habit.

'Then it must be pretty spectacular from the top,' commented Chris. 'What is it like and how much further is it?'

'Haven't the faintest idea,' replied Habit. 'I've never seen the point in going right to the top. And why should I bother? I know this ground well now and it suits me just fine.'

'Well surely it's worth going up some time or other?' asked Chris.

'I've often thought about it,' answered Habit, 'but each time I do, it always seems to be such an effort to actually do so.'

'Can I ask where you're from and where you are heading then?' said Chris.

'Certainly but first would you like a cup of coffee or something? I have it all fairly organised here nowadays, you know.'

Chris was pleased to be offered a drink, gratefully accepted and settled back into the soft carpet of grass to enjoy it.

'I started out from Familiar Town in the State of Mediocrity,' began Habit.

'That's the same State I started out from,' interrupted Chris.

Looking out at the view before him, Habit seemed to ignore the interruption and continued talking.

'Though *I* actually had no intention of ever leaving, it was my girlfriend, Curious, who persuaded me to do so. She had apparently heard about some Land called Prosperity and wanted to visit it. Well, I had got used to being in her company, so her suggestion to go there together seemed like a good idea at the time. It was hard to leave though let me tell you, because I have always striven to remain consistent with what I am most familiar with, and to act differently, well it just didn't feel right.'

'So where is Curious now?' asked Chris.

'Well, if you give me a chance, I'll get to that. It's my story you know, so you'll have to let me tell it the way I always do!' replied Habit.

'Anyway,' he continued again, 'we came to this gate—'

'Would that be Change Border?' put in Chris who was so excited to hear about the path he himself had taken. The look that Habit gave him however spoke volumes. 'Sorry,' he mumbled.

'*Anyway*, it may well have been what you say, but as we couldn't find anyone in attendance, Curious decided that we should duck under the barrier and just go through. Well, we did that, which let me tell you did not rest easy with me at all. However, we came upon this path marked the Road of Inclination, which was a nice road and suited us both and it led straight to this hill. We decided to take the middle of the three-road junction at the bottom of the hill, simply because it was the middle one, which is something I have always done and we reached this point.'

Habit paused for some coffee and though Chris wanted to ask something, thought better of interrupting him.

> Getting out of your comfort zone and leaving behind your old negative habits will lead you to discover the new positive you.

'Anyway, I didn't like it coming up this hill at first but when I reached this place it reminded me of home, so I soon warmed to it. But Curious wouldn't settle. She suggested that, as the road ahead was getting steeper, she would go back down and check out where the other roads led. So, as we were getting on each other's nerves a bit, I stayed here and she went to investigate. And that's how I came to be here. Lucky old me to find this place, that's what I say. Don't you agree?'

'Well, you do seem to be stuck halfway from nowhere to somewhere, if you don't mind me saying,' said Chris. 'But what about Curious, don't you ever feel like going to find her?'

'Not at all. She's always done things like that ever since I've known her. I just wish I didn't allow myself to be persuaded by her all the time. Just can't help myself I suppose. No, she will be all right, I'm sure. But I certainly don't see myself as "stuck" here, as you say. Far from it. I'm very comfortable here. Could I expect anything more? No, I'm pleased where I am today and I intend to stay just where I am. Another coffee?'

'I believe that it's more a matter of realising our potential, not just satisfaction of our needs,' said Chris. 'For my part, I stand to deliver. To deliver better-than-excellent service. And in learning to do so I will receive greater-than-expected rewards.'

Habit turned from the view before him and looked at Chris as if he were from another planet.

'Better-than-excellent service?' Habit said. 'But why? In Familiar Town the service is what I've always been used to. Why would I want it to be any different?'

'Perhaps the service is very good there, then,' said Chris. 'Perhaps better than the City of Apathy where I come from.'

'Well, I did visit that big City once and I don't remember the service there being any different from what I was familiar with,' replied Habit.

'Then don't you mind poor service?' asked Chris.

'It's not a question of minding,' said Habit, 'it's a matter of what a person gets used to. Take me, I'm in the wholesale furnishing industry. We fulfil the orders for retail outlets. We don't have to worry about service too much though because of the system we operate.'

'What system?' enquired Chris.

'The order system of course,' answered Habit. 'Someone chooses a suite of furniture from a retail outlet. They pay something to secure it, although it doesn't actually exist yet. But their payment means we can start to make it. Our system allows delivery to be between six and twelve weeks. Sometimes, because of a backlog of orders, we don't start making it for twelve weeks. But the furniture doesn't take long to make and the customer doesn't seem to mind the extra time because they're just pleased to get it. Unless, of course, they get the wrong one or it's not been put together properly. But even if that happens the system always allows them to change it, though there would be a further waiting period.'

> Customers should never have to 'get used to' poor service. It should be something that they never encounter in the first place.

'And are your customers happy with that system?' asked Chris.

'Well, no one has ever complained before, though they're not really our customers, are they? Anyway, even if they do complain I don't see how it would be down to us. Our job is to meet the orders, not to take them.'

'But surely the order takers liaise with you?'

'What and lose their sale!' exclaimed Habit. 'Why would they want to do that? That wouldn't help the industry would it, and with it getting so competitive it's hard enough as it is. Anyway, why should the customer complain? We make furniture that sells anyway. The customer doesn't have to buy. Another coffee?'

'But following that system surely you stand the risk of having no customers,' said Chris.

'There will always be customers!' replied Habit. 'That is not the difficulty today. No, the difficulty comes when they challenge the way things are done. Things for which they should be grateful.'

'What do you mean exactly?' asked Chris.

'Take my friend, Routine,' said Habit. 'Now, *he* understands all about how important business is to customers. He's a bank manager. He has quite rightly got his customers to accept that they need the services his bank provides. But would you believe that some customers have argued that the bank needs them! How can a bank need them, after all it's the bank that has the money people want, not the other way about.'

'Well, it's an interesting concept, though I can't say I agree with you,' said Chris. 'Let's face it, the bank wouldn't exist without customers.'

'You may say that, but I don't like upsetting my bank. If I did I would probably not be able to get any money out of one of those machines in the wall just when I need it. *Anyway*, the point I'm making is that Routine received a complaint from a customer who had been waiting for the bank to open. Well, the bank always opens at nine thirty and one morning it was pouring with rain. There was quite a queue of people and apparently they could all see bank staff inside waiting for the door to open. Some customers banged on the door at nine twenty-five but it wouldn't open. When it did open, at the right time let me tell you, one soaked customer asked why they couldn't have opened the door earlier on this occasion. Routine said he couldn't because it was bank policy, and they couldn't just change policy because it was raining.

'This answer didn't satisfy this customer. Routine told me that the customer visited the head office. Apparently, some bright spark replied that the opening time was not a policy, but a guideline for the manager to follow at his discretion.'

'So what happened,' asked Chris. 'Did Routine apologise?'

'Far from it,' said Habit. 'And the customer closed his account and went elsewhere. Which goes to show that we need banks more than they need us but, and more importantly, if you can't stick to a routine what on earth are you left with in life? Another coffee?'

Chris couldn't be bothered to reason with Habit. 'If I wasn't so tired I would,' he thought. And the longer Chris stayed in the comfort zone with Habit the more reluctant he was inclined to get started again. Weary after his initial climb and so relaxed looking at the view, he fell asleep. As he did so the Motive Certificate that Inspiration had given to him fell from his jacket and rolled away. When he woke up he saw he was alone and that it was already early evening.

'How could I have been so stupid to rest for so long?' he chastised himself. 'It will be dark before I get to the top now and I still have to find Integrity House.'

Rushing up the hill, driven more by his annoyance with himself than anything else, he was nearing the top when he saw two people making their way down the hill as fast as they could. The name of one was Suspicion and the name of the other was Criticism, of whom Chris asked, 'Why are you going down the hill in such a hurry?'

'Because the path ahead is dangerous, so there is little point in going ahead.'

'But this is the way to Integrity House, isn't it?' asked Chris. 'What are you running away from?'

'The infamous bandits, Bureaucrat and Administrate, who attack unsuspecting travellers in these parts,' said Suspicion, 'we have reason to believe that they are on the rampage tonight.'

'And we don't want them to harm us,' added Suspicion. 'Might I ask why you are about so late in the day? Are you a scout for them?'

'Of course not!' shouted Chris, beginning to feel afraid. 'I am on my way to Service City and have been advised by Inspiration to rest at Integrity House. I am simply guilty of falling asleep in the comfort zone for too long.'

'Then you'll hardly be welcome at Integrity House. They won't have any time for sluggards such as you,' said Criticism. 'Perhaps you'd better turn back.'

'And perhaps you should ask yourself why these outrageous bandits lie so close to Integrity House. Perhaps they are all in business together, eh?' added Suspicion.

'But how can you be certain such bandits are loose?' asked Chris.

'Do we look stupid or something?' said Suspicion continuing to make his way down the hill. 'A person has to be on their guard in life you know.'

'And it's clear to see that you're one of those people that people guard themselves against,' added Criticism following behind him. 'It strikes me that you're wasting your time heading for Service City for, mark my words, you'll find little comfort ahead of you and the likes of you will be turned away.'

Chris was left alone feeling somewhat fearful about what lay ahead. Furthermore, he felt quite discouraged and down-hearted about his whole trip. So, seeking encouragement from the charter that Inspiration had given him, he felt for it in his coat.

'It's not there!' he cried out loud to himself. 'How could I have been so careless as to lose it?' And, realising that it must have fallen from him when he was in the comfort zone, started to make his way back to it.

'How stupid to do such a thing that will make me retrace my steps and do this part of my journey three times! And how will I find my charter in this gathering dark? But without it how will I remind myself of what I am about? Of what is important to me? Of what I am resolved to do? There is nothing to do but to find it.'

> You must not regard your personal mission
> statement lightly. Reread it and carry it with
> you as a constant reminder to support you.

Reaching the comfort zone he searched frantically around where he had rested. Nothing. 'It must be nearby,' he thought and telling himself to stay calm, he searched again, methodically. His concentrated effort paid off and with relief he saw his charter jutting out from the undergrowth. Gratefully he seized it and read its contents. Reminding himself of his mission encouraged him and he once more set off up the hill with a determined pace. 'I will not be put off my course just because of what someone says,' he told himself. 'If there is danger ahead, then I will deal with it when I come to it!'

It was dark when Chris reached the top of the hill for the second time and he once more chastised himself for resting so long and for being careless. 'I have even missed the opportunity of seeing the view from up here as well as arriving at Integrity House in the safety of daylight.'

In the distance he could make out a clear light within a building and immediately made towards it. As he did so he heard some distressed cries.

'I must be bold,' he encouraged himself, 'and keep going. It's not far now. I'll be there in just a short time.'

Coming upon what seemed to him to be the beginning of an entrance, he was relieved to see the sign Integrity House. At the same time, however, the shouts were becoming louder. They were cries for help. Straining his eyes to see further down the entrance he could just make out two figures.

'Well, faint heart never served anyone,' he muttered to himself and went closer.

'Help us,' said Bureaucrat, 'for my colleague and I have been caught in a trap.'

Chris could now discern that the person who spoke and his colleague were in what appeared to be an utter tangle of red tape that stuck to them like glue.

'You are indeed,' said Chris, 'but I sense that it is a trap of your own making. And tell me how you think I can help you for I suspect that doing so will only leave me as tied up as you are.'

'That's what I told him when he asked me to help!' cried Administrate. 'The fool used far too much tape, much more than was necessary—'

'Be quiet, you idiot!' cursed Bureaucrat. 'If it wasn't for your bungling supervision this would never have happened!' And turning to Chris, said in more pleasant terms, 'If you would be kind enough to get us out of our unfortunate predicament, I can assure you that it is within my power to smooth the way ahead for you.'

'And under what authority would that be?' enquired Chris.

'Under the authority invested in me by the State of Limbo, a land which lies ahead of you and one that you indeed may have to cross.'

'And I would be more than happy to arrange a transit visa and pass for you,' added Administrate, 'for a small fee, of course, though I am more than happy to discount this for you in return for your assistance.'

'You have been clearly hoisted by your own petard,' mused Chris, 'and I wonder how much of this red tape you were intending to use to entrap me. I'll tell you what I will do. As you are in your fix in the entrance of Integrity House, and I know that I alone could not free you, I will inform the residents straight away. They will know what to do.'

'Wait,' called Bureaucrat, as Chris left them and walked towards the house. Ignoring their pleas, Chris knocked on the door.

Inside Integrity House Chris met with Probity, who lived there along with his two sisters, Prudence and Patience. After being welcomed, Chris apologised for being late and explained why. He then explained the predicament of Bureaucrat and Administrate at their entrance.

'I have to admit to being very afraid when I met them, after I learned that they were bandits,' said Chris.

'Certainly, they are infamous for preying on the nerves of people,' replied Probity, 'but they are not really bandits.'

'But you were right to leave them, as we will do, for a while,' said Patience. 'For they must learn to desist from holding up so many who pass by here.'

'Yes, we'll cut them free in the morning,' added Prudence. 'Though it won't be for the first time we have had to do so, and I'm afraid it won't be the last.'

'But it *is* good to hear that you confronted your fears and in doing so overcame them,' said Probity. 'Having courage is not the absence of fear, rather it is the mastery of it.'

'And the more you face what frightens you, the more mastery you acquire,' said Patience.

'And the more honest you are about why you are afraid, the more you are able to face what frightens you,' put in Prudence. 'But come now, it's late and you must be both hungry and tired. Tomorrow we can talk.'

Facing up to what scares you will show you how to overcome your fears. Courage comes from mastering your fears.

Upon waking the following morning Chris took a few moments to reflect on his conversation with Inspiration and once more read his Charter. 'It's great to feel such a sense of belonging,' he said to himself. 'When every step I take is guided by what I believe is really important to me, it makes every step worthwhile, even an adventure.'

A short time later, fully refreshed from his good night's sleep, he joined his three hosts.

'Good morning,' said Probity brightly. 'You'll be interested to know that we've freed your *acquaintances* from last night. Not that they realise it yet as they are both still fast asleep.'

'Yes, it's always easier that way,' joined in Prudence. 'Otherwise we only put ourselves at risk. They always seem to be intent on tying us up in knots with them in their eagerness to get out.'

'They'll no doubt wake up when they're good and ready and go off and plan what they're going to do next,' said Patience. 'They always do.'

'So,' said Probity, gazing at Chris, 'I see that you carry good arms and a charter for guidance. It is good to see that you have kept to the path. I take it that you are heading towards Service City?'

'Yes, though I'm afraid that there is a lot for me to learn before entering it,' said Chris.

'And why is that?' asked Probity.

'Because even after my time with Accountability and his colleagues, I allowed myself to get stuck in the comfort zone with Habit. I found that I lacked the fortitude to argue with Habit about his order systems and his story of Routine, and I was even careless enough to lose the charter that Inspiration had instructed me to keep safe.'

'You must learn to forgive yourself,' said Patience. 'You are human, not a machine and it is the conditioned nature of Man

89

to do such things. It takes time to build up new habits that will ensure the success of your mission.'

'But it's important that you keep your mind on what *is* important to you, added Probity. And in fairness to yourself you did something about your error as soon as you realised. You went back to retrieve what was important and were rewarded by finding it.'

'And that was after you had met with Criticism and Suspicion, who caused you to become fearful of the path you were travelling on,' said Prudence. 'They are often to be found loitering at the top of the Hill of Reluctance, seeking to talk to travellers who have managed to get to the top. You were lucky they were in a hurry, because the tongues of those two can be more damaging than the danger they warned was before you.'

'But what is important is that you *are* now here,' said Probity. 'For *here* you will learn that the function of integrity is to reflect on the beliefs, values and principles of every individual both personally and professionally.'

'And with this ability you will be able to look upon people like Habit with tolerance,' said Patience. 'For we know of Habit also, and although he appears stuck in his ways there are good things about him, too. After all, however he was persuaded, he *has* made it halfway up the Hill of Reluctance.'

To ensure a mission's success, first build the required success habits.

'He was persuaded by his girlfriend, Curious,' said Chris.

'It usually does take an outside influence for Habit to do something different to what he has always done,' replied Patience, 'but unfortunately it is rarely permanent, unless he is able to decide for himself. Changing something about ourselves because we want to will always be of more benefit to us than changing because another has persuaded us to. Once Habit no longer feels satisfaction for what he is doing or where he is, he will want to alter his view of things to seek greater satisfaction.'

'So, he will be able to change then and perhaps move forward?' asked Chris.

'It depends on the level of satisfaction that he gets for continuing to do what he does. If he is unsure as to whether his satisfaction will increase, then he will prefer to stick to what he knows. If what he is familiar with starts to give him more pain than pleasure, then the chances of him replacing an old tendency with a new one are good.'

'Most of what Habit does is a reaction, though for most of the time he thinks what he does is just instinctive,' said Probity. 'And his reactions have been brought about because of repetition. That is why so much of what he does is second nature. It has become so through repetition. Now, repetition in itself is neither a bad thing, nor a good thing. In truth it is a learning tool but most of the time people use it to debilitate themselves rather than use it for growth.'

Changing through personal choice is better than through external pressure.

'Take imagination, for example,' said Prudence. 'It is at our disposal to create our dreams. Yet, many people misuse it for the disposal of their dreams.'

'But how can imagination bring about our dreams?' asked Chris.

'Because nothing can be materially accomplished without first being mentally created, so if we can learn to use it more proactively, instead of reactively, we benefit enormously. When repetitively used, imagination actually makes our dreams more real, more concrete. Conversely, and if we allow it, our fears become more real too.'

'Keeping our mind on what we want to happen, instead of fretting over what we don't want to happen is what we need to do then,' said Chris.

'Correct,' said Prudence.

'But what about Habit's friend Routine,' said Chris. 'He was religious about keeping his mind and actions on what he believed to be right, even at the expense of actually losing a customer.'

'People will always feel secure when they have a set format to follow,' replied Probity. 'Indeed, some will consider the security of everything they hold dear in the comfort of a traditional policy. That is why some people look to point out where others go wrong in not adhering to such a policy. Why, some will even take pleasure in it. Routine was misguided at the outset by one of the commonest myths in offering service to others. He put his own interests, and what he perceived as his bank's interests, before the interests of one of his customers. Integrity, however, requires putting your customers' interests before your own.'

Use your imagination as a positive tool to keep your inspirations real and achievable.

'I really believe that,' said Chris. 'Yet, so many businesses that claim in their marketing a policy of putting customers first, seldom seem to ever follow through.'

'That's usually because as a marketing initiative it sounds good, and of course works in the short term,' said Probity. 'But the reality is that such promises cause resentment when they remain undelivered. Integrity, in the individual or company, must be reflected in the service actions, which customers feel values them. And in order to be able to deliver profitable service to the customer, it is important to show them that you value what they want more than you value what you do. Both their time and their interest are more important than your time and interests. In which case, you have to know what is important to you.'

'I know what is important to me,' said Chris. 'My customers are important to me and I stand to deliver what they want.'

> Show your customers that you value them and that their time is more important to you than your time.

'Those are indeed fine words and the enthusiasm that you recite them with makes me believe that you will follow them through,' said Probity. 'For make no mistake, customers don't like being let down when they have been promised that something will happen. They resent being told how fantastic a particular service is, having to wait for it and then being told that such a service is worth waiting for. They feel duped when exciting advertisements offer fantastic service and they are unable to either get through on the phone, or, when they finally do, the person on the other end is too busy, indifferent, disinterested, not aware of the offer just started or even rude.

'Integrity is delivering what you promise, saying what you mean and meaning what you say. Therefore everyone that serves another must be aware of the values that are important to him or her and the values that are important to the company. With such knowledge they can then emotionalise them for the benefit of customer and business alike. Because for a business vehicle to be driven by values it must make certain that all its passengers are in their seats and are prepared to put their own genuine emotions into showing the customers how much they value them.'

Integrity is keeping your promises, being honest and sincere to your customers.

'You have already learned that the essential prerequisite, even before being able to consider giving better-than-excellent service, is continuous improvement of the individual through persistent personal development,' said Patience.

'I have indeed,' said Chris. 'And the importance of aligning what you are with what you do through evaluating motives, and establishing a personal mission.'

'Then you will have by now realised that fulfilling your aim of better-than-excellent service cannot be treated as something that can be ticked off on a simple to-do list.'

Absolutely, and I understand that my potential will only ever be realised through my commitment to continually stretching myself with greater and more challenging goals,' replied Chris.

'Well here lies the difficulty that business does not fully recognise when it promises to put customers first. Although every individual who seeks entry into Service City has a personal responsibility to work at being the best they can be for themselves, every business has a fundamental responsibility to do something too. Every business must school character.'

'What do you mean, school character?' asked Chris.

'The majority of people spend a greater portion of their life at work than at school,' continued Patience. 'School teaches us many of life's basics, but it is not until we are interacting with others that we are able to hone and improve our basic skills, discover and utilise many others and have the opportunity to become what we are truly capable of.

'Our biggest growth will always come from our character development, but it is our competency that business is more interested in. Consequently, training budgets favour competency skills in the belief that greater competency will bring about greater profit. Business understands automation and integrated systems and prefers their smooth operation to autonomy and initiative. Business would no doubt argue against this but the way the training budget is spent will tell a different story. For the former elements are competency based, while the latter are character based. Almost all the budget and a significant number of meetings, which involve immense manpower, are on improving the systems. Periodically, and when under pressure to do something about a bad work ethos and lack of communication, business will consider some character schooling, do it and then tick it off as done.

> Character schooling through quick-fix courses is not efficient or lasting. Providing an atmosphere that aids learning is a permanent benefit to the company because it creates a harmonious staff.

'Yet, in providing the opportunity to continually improve people through becoming a learning organisation, business will ensure greater profitable growth, more loyal customers and a harmonious unified environment. The duty to treat their staff as customers who like them so that their employees in turn can duplicate such ethos with customers, is common to all business leaders in Service City.'

'I wish that it were the case where I come from,' said Chris. 'But I know that such a suggestion would be met with the concern that the business would merely be training people to leave them and start in competition against them.'

'There is a tendency for that viewpoint whenever the idea, action or follow-through for such schooling is half-hearted or given lip service,' said Probity. 'People will not buy into something unless they can see that what is offered is for the benefit of all and not just good for the business. Conducted properly, a business can stay unified with loyal employees who enjoy increasing success because of their unified efforts. In so doing, success is continuously built on the success of others. Just imagine for a moment the vast resources of untapped potential within the members of a company. Without developing the confidence for people to do what they are truly capable off, or the character to harness what they can do, a business is not mining the diamonds it has within it.'

'In my city many businesses tell their employees that they are its greatest asset, but the employees don't really believe it,' said Chris.

> Building character and developing confidence
> through personal development can be the
> only successful way to release the untapped
> potential of people.

'Well, that's probably just as well anyway, because it isn't the case,' said Probity. 'Employees are not a business's greatest asset, though certainly they are important to what is.'

'If it's not people then what is it?' asked a perplexed Chris.

'Why, customers of course!' said Probity. 'Without customers a business would not even exist. There would be no people as there would be no requirement for them. Cash flow is not the life blood of a business, customers are, for without them there is no cash flow, there is nothing.'

'So when a business fails it is not because of cash flow then, it's because of lack of custom,' said Chris.

'If you don't provide what people want, then no amount of cash flow will help,' put in Prudence. 'Often people will provide something and then try to market it, blaming marketing and poor sales for bad performance. After all, they will say, we know the product is good. The product may be the best invention since sliced bread, but if every customer around you prefers rice, what good will it do you? What is required is a full understanding of what customers want to experience, a true empathy for them. Take quality, which can only ever be subjective. Many businesses will pride themselves on the quality of the service they provide. But customers don't buy because of quality. They buy because of the quality they *perceive* they are getting.'

'So, understanding what customers want is about learning to understand how *they*, the customer, perceive things,' said Chris.

'Exactly!' said Probity. 'And this is a major point to understand, because perceptions relate to people's frame of reference. Our perceptions dictate how we react or respond to the things we see or are offered. They dictate our values and beliefs, which is why it is important for business to see things in the same way that their customers do.'

'How is it possible to do that, though?' asked Chris.

'Through simply putting yourself in their shoes,' answered Probity. 'Take any hotel in Service City, for example. All the people who are involved experience the hotel as if they are a customer. Both the engineer and the housekeeper will then know at first hand if the shower unit really works, as it should. The receptionist will know what it is like to make a reservation, be put on hold, called back, assisted and welcomed. The cashiers will experience first hand what it is like when they come to settle a bill. The restaurant employees will experience what it is like to book, wait, be served, eat and be treated. All personnel will acquire an understanding of what it is like *to be* a customer at their hotel. They will be able to perceive as the customer does, and in so doing, will perceive their role and the customer's role more clearly.'

'But surely they would get different treatment anyway

because they work there and their colleagues would be conscious of why they are there,' said Chris. 'And how could they be expected to pay for their stay when it was for the sake of the customer?'

'Well, first there is an understanding between hotels in Service City so that employees can stay at different hotels and find out what it is like to be a customer. What they experience assists their perception of the customer experience. When they stay at their own hotel their experience will then tell them if they are getting special treatment because of who they are, or if the service is the way it always is. Also, their colleagues recognise the importance of the learning experience so everyone benefits. Secondly, it is a proven fact that people do not value that which they receive for nothing. The hotels in Service City therefore provide an additional allowance for character development, such as learning the customer experience, which is considered extremely valuable. The employee does not have to use it, but in doing so, it is a clear indication that he or she shares the values that the hotel stands by, and is committed to his future development.'

Perception of the customer experience is the vital key to developing long lasting, loyal relationships.

'So understanding the customer experience is something that hotels in Service City highly value,' said Chris.

'It is certainly considered the vital key in developing long lasting loyal relationships with the growing number of clientele.'

'I can't wait to experience such service,' said Chris. 'The last few hotels that I have stayed in are so busy dealing with customers they never have time to serve them. I believe that some really do make an effort to do what they can. But it is based on their perception of what should be done, rather than on their experience of what could be done. I recall my own experience at a hotel where I once commented that the shower in my en-suite room was not functioning correctly. Though they appreciated the information and promised to repair it, upon my return I discovered the same thing in a different room. When I asked at reception if all the rooms were perhaps the same, I was told that the engineers were always complaining that housekeeping never kept them informed of difficulties. But reception would pass on the comment anyway.'

'Then you see the importance of character development in addition to simple competency; of the importance of perceiving what the customer wants through understanding their experience; and of not putting your own interest before those of whom you are serving,' said Probity. 'When our father, Integrity and our mother, Trust, first built this house it was very much for their aim that these elements should be at the very core of both individual and organisational values. They considered that the best way to show your customers how much you value them was through keeping whatever promises you made to them. My sisters and I are committed to sharing these values with travellers who are intent on seeking Service City. For we, like our parents, acknowledge that gaining the rewards of success and wealth that Service City promises, requires greater adherence to such values, because of the additional responsibility that such rewards bring with them.'

'I am indeed grateful for the generous hospitality that you have extended to me,' said Chris. 'And I earnestly promise that I will apply the wisdom you have shared with me.'

'Your sincerity is clearly genuine,' said Prudence. 'And I only wish that what we have shared with you could serve you as well on your journey to Service City as it will when you are there.

Sadly, though, there are trials ahead of you that only your own resilience can overcome. But never forget that so long as you do not question your resolve, your resilience will *always* overcome. For providence moves on the side of a genuine resolve.

'There is one gift we do have for you, however, to add to the arms you have already received. Something that will help you hold firm to your values through thick and thin and allow your honour to shine through for all to see. It is the Breastplate of Proof of *who* you are and it will protect your heart should the valley ahead of you prove challenging.'

'Well,' said Probity getting up and walking towards the door, 'to my mind, though you have a long way ahead, you are now well prepared and have a strong resolve. Come, sisters, let us walk with our guest to beyond our gate.'

'Is it possible that you can tell me how far Service City is, or the Land of Prosperity?' enquired Chris as they reached the Gate.

'By continuing on your path you can be certain that you will come to it, and that you will recognise it when you do so,' replied Probity. 'I cannot tell you how long it will take, though from where we are now you may just be able to discern the Ground of Good Fortune in the far distance.'

Chris looked in the direction that Probity was pointing and could just make out a high ridge of land that, bathed as it was in sunlight, appeared golden. 'From that point you will be able to see Service City,' continued Probity.

Chris's heart rose with excitement at being able to see where he was heading, even though it was so faint in the distance. 'Have any others passed by here recently who are trying to reach the same destination?' he asked.

'Indeed, a good man passed by this way not long before you,' replied Probity.

'Did you know him at all?' asked Chris.

'We asked his name,' said Prudence, ' and he told us it was Self-Reliance.'

'I have heard of him!' said Chris. 'He comes from where I was originally born. We used to be friends as small children, but I remember he moved away a long time ago. How far ahead of me do you think he will be?'

'With a determined step you may be able to catch up with him, as you are certainly on the same road,' answered Patience. 'Good luck.'

'Yes, good luck and keep your resolve firm in crossing the valley that lies ahead of you,' said Probity. 'The path can be slippery and precarious, so keep true to each of your steps.'

To Be a Pilgrim ...

- Inspire yourself with what you stand for
- Make a difference in the lives of others by improving your own life first
- Beware of habits that distract you from your path
- Always face up to what frightens you
- Keep your mind on what is important to you, do not fret over what is not
- Integrity in service requires putting customers' interests before your own
- Continually stretch yourself with greater and more challenging goals
- Never question your resolve, and you will always overcome

Chapter Four

Crossing the Valley of Embarrassment

Chris felt good. Even dressed with the armour that had been given to him he had never felt so light of step. 'My burden of frustration must have weighed me down much more than I ever realised,' he thought. 'Isn't it strange how it is not until a self-inflicted burden has gone that you appreciate how much more enjoyable life is without it. And what's also strange is how these gifts of armour seem to be of no weight at all. It's almost as if they have become part of me, while at the same time making me stronger, and more confident.'

As he made his way down the slippery slope before him, which was the Valley of Embarrassment, Chris was careful to watch his step, as Probity advised. But with his charter safe behind his Breastplate of Proof, he felt full of determination. A determination that had been further fuelled by having seen the Ground of Good Fortune. Admittedly, it had only been a glimpse and was not his ultimate destination. But none the less it was still a key part of where he was heading and when you are able to see where you are going it makes you more resolved to get there. 'How fortunate I am to know where I am going!' our pilgrim said out loud to himself. 'And with every possibility of meeting Self-Reliance on the path, what more could I wish for?'

'That depends on where you really *ought* to be going,' said a voice to his side. 'What on earth do you think you are doing so far from where you should be?'

Turning quickly to the clearing at his side Chris was horrified to see the most hideous monster. Chris could see that its skin was full of tension as if stretched in knots. As for its eyes, they looked as though they were set in stone, for their cold gaze lacked any emotion. Its enormous limbs outstretched, threatening to crush all that was around it. And it seemed to Chris that from its mouth spat shards of ice.

'Stay away from me, whatever you are!' shouted Chris in alarm.

'Now that's not very grateful of you after I have gone out of my way specifically to find you,' boomed Securi-I-tas. 'Tell me, where have you come from and where are you going?'

Fear rose in Chris's mind as he realised that the creature before him was the same one he had hoped he would *not* meet. His immediate thought was whether he should flee from it, or stand his ground. 'I want to run from this fiendish creature,' he said to himself. 'Yet with no armour to protect my back, how will I defend myself from its attack if it chases me? No, it is better that I stand my ground, for if I don't do that then what is my life about?'

Overcoming his immediate fear, Chris felt calmer and said, 'I am quite prepared indeed to answer your questions. For I am pleased with my progress. I have recently quit the City of Apathy within Mediocrity and am bound for Service City that lies within Prosperity.'

'What gives you the audacity to take such a journey? And the impertinence to leave without my permission?' snapped Securi-I-tas. 'Don't you know that I rule the World of Mediocrity and I despise it when one of my subjects attempts to leave? How is it that you run away from your king?'

'Because there is a worthier king I am eager to serve and, by choosing to do so, I will be allowed to release my full potential,' replied Chris.

'Serve another?' hissed Securi-I-tas threateningly. 'Were it not for the hope that you will return to me, I would strike you down now! But listen; come back to my kingdom of your own free will. For my part, I promise to reward you with greater privileges than you would ever receive at this Service City you speak of. You have no idea how the realms of my kingdom can benefit you over time.'

'Ah, but I do,' said Chris. 'Because I have known many of your subjects who have allowed you to rule them for all of their lives and without exception they have lost the will to rule themselves.'

'Of course and why would *I* want it to be any different!' said Securi-I-tas. 'For what better way is there? I rule them and in the knowledge that I do, they find comfort. Make no mistake, security is what *everyone* wants and *I* am the only one who can provide it. Consider the many forms of security that are available for people when they follow me.'

'The only security you offer is a false sense of security,' argued Chris defiantly. 'One that can only result in making a person feel insecure.'

'Nonsense! How can you believe such a thing? Whenever people want the security of a status, title or role, I give it to them. Whenever they want it in the form of possessions, a car, or better house, I give it to them. What other ruler could be so munificent? Certainly not the King in Service City! That sanctimonious ruler will never be satisfied. He lives to complain. Come, take the opportunity to return to my sovereignty before it is too late.'

'Opportunity? How can the security you talk about be an opportunity?' scoffed Chris. 'I have already learned that the only real security is within the soul of the individual who chooses to take personal responsibility for where he has been, where he is now and where he is going. Nothing external can ever provide a permanent sense of security internally. Indeed, reliance for what lies outside of us can only ever create insecurity. To my mind, only a firm resolve to fulfil my potential can provide meaningful security for me.'

'Ha!' snarled Securi-I-tas. 'What resolve? Is that the resolve that got you stuck in the Pub of Procrastination? Is that the resolve that drove you to continuously ask others how you could shed your burden, when all you had to do was ask me? Is that the resolve that caused you to fall asleep so easily in the comfort zone? To lose your charter almost as soon as you were given it? To consider turning back because bandits were ahead of you? Ha! Some resolve! Do you think that this Land of Prosperity you talk of will tolerate such a "resolve"? Why don't you just stop deluding yourself! On the other hand, do I make such demands of you? Not at all! All *I* ask is for you to *not* try to be someone you're *not*. Why do you think I have come searching for you?'

'Because you gain your own power from the insecurities of men!' said Chris. 'It may be true that my resolve was not firm at the outset and I freely admit that I am guilty of being faint-hearted. That was because, until recently, I didn't know myself, didn't know my capabilities, let alone even believe in myself.

Whenever you meet adversity that knocks you back, your only security is belief in yourself.

'Under your rule I never even considered evaluating myself or really understanding what my motives could possibly be. I was too busy evaluating others in case they threatened my security. I had no real idea about what was important to me, or indeed what I stood for. I was more concerned about being able to pigeonhole others so that I could get a handle on them. But that was before I realised that you can only truly recognise the motives of others when you are sure of your own. And I don't believe that my future is simply an extension of my past. Just because I have made mistakes, does not make me a mistake. Just because I have failed, does not make me a failure. In pursuing my course my resolve has become firmer, my belief in myself is stronger, my confidence in myself is greater. My self-respect and integrity are my security now and the only security I'll ever need. That is what is asked of me to enter Service City, for the King there knows that with his people I am able to serve others to the best of my ability. Living under your rule offers no more than becoming my own worst enemy!'

With that Securi-I-tas broke into a dreadful rage saying, 'I despise the ideas that you have been clearly brainwashed with. This *King* you talk of is a false ruler, one that demands a sense of freedom in place of servility. How can people feel secure if they are free to do what they want for others? Without confinement there can only be anarchy. Such philosophy can only threaten my existence, which I will not tolerate!'

Chris could see that the time to fight the menace before him had finally come. It seemed to him that in making the decision to stand his ground against Securi-I-tas, his apparel began to change. The Mettle Gauntlets that Enthusiasm had given him grew firm on his hands, as one went to draw the Sword of Steadfastness, received from Persistence, and the other raised the Shield of Sequence, that Discipline had given him. Both the Helmet of Conscience and the Breastplate of Proof, given respectively by Accountability and Prudence, began to shine in the daylight.

Momentarily surprised by the firmness of the growing

resolve witnessed before him, Securi-I-tas then began to deal blow after blow upon Chris. His shield, raised to protect him from such fearsome attack, deflected each one in turn. But, having never experienced such a frightening attack before, it was all Chris could do to just lean on his sword for support. In addition to the blows, Securi-I-tas spat terrifying darts of ice at him from his mouth, wounding Chris's arms and legs. Chris began to feel a rising sense of panic inside him.

'What am I doing?' he thought in despair. 'This monster is intent on destroying me rather than letting me go! Why couldn't I have just said what it wanted to hear? Why did I have to fight when I have no way of winning?'

Just then Chris heard a voice inside reminding him to, 'Never forget that so long as you do not question your resolve, your resilience will *always* overcome. For providence moves on the side of a genuine resolve.'

'Yes,' repeated Chris, 'just what am I doing questioning my resolve in the midst of a battle, when there can be only one way forward!' And with that he raised his sword and fought fiercely back, trading blow for blow.

The battle continued for half a day but, despite almost everything inside screaming at him to give up, Chris kept up his fight. Then, with his energy nearing exhaustion, Securi-I-tas struck a vicious blow that caused Chris to lose his footing and slip to the ground, and as he did so his sword fell from his hand.

'You see!' shouted Securi-I-tas in triumph, 'I'm sure of you now,' and with that he made ready to crush Chris with his final blow.

Drawing on his last ounce of resolve Chris reached for his fallen sword, grasped it, turned and shouted back, 'I will never give up to you,' and plunged it into his oncoming assailant. 'My steadfastness is the measure of my belief in myself! And it doesn't involve you!' shouted Chris as he thrust his deadly blade up to the hilt.

Letting out a hideous roar Securi-I-tas fell back. Then with a venomous look of resentment the monster fled. Chris never saw it again.

Flying to the aid of a genuine resolve, Providence itself had moved.

Chris did not know how long he lay on the ground in his exhausted state. As he began to come around he felt nauseous and ached all over. Physically, emotionally and mentally drained, he was momentarily uncertain what had happened. Then, with a start, he suddenly realised, 'That monster that I was so concerned about meeting, I did come face to face with! And I fought it! And though it almost overcame and crushed me, I defeated it!'

He sensed an inner calm that he had not experienced before. All his previous fears about what might happen were gone. He no longer felt as though his security lay in the opinion of others.

'How ridiculous to have previously concerned myself with what other people think of me? How can it be any of my business what others think? I can't get inside their head. The frame of reference that dictates how they may perceive me is not within my control. There is only one thing in my control and that is *my* thinking. How can I control their thinking? What right have I got to do so anyway?

'It is *so* clear to me now that at any one time each of us is either in control of our lives, or not in control of it. There are no halfway measures. Whenever I react to another because what they say bothers me, I am giving them control over my emotions. Whenever I do not react to what they say, but respond to what I feel is right, guided by what is important to me, I maintain command over my thinking. If I can't control my thinking what is my life worth? If I can't have command over my thoughts how will I have command over my actions? My security is within me, knowing what I want and keeping my mind on what I want. Knowing that *what* I want is *what* I am to do, because of the importance I feel about it. If I hadn't been so concerned about meeting Securi-I-tas, the monster would never have challenged me in the first place. I sought the battle out myself, just as it was predicted that I might. But I overcame the fears that I attracted! I kept my resolve and won through my worst fears.

'How wrong I have been to worry about security, when it only exists in our fears. A person can work the whole of their lifetime with just a few words separating them from security and insecurity, between employment and unemployment: "You're fired, you're redundant," or "I'm sorry." Civilisations don't have futures. Countries don't have futures. Companies don't have futures. It is the people that form the companies, countries and civilisations that have futures. Civilisations can grow, plateau and fall away. They can last a thousand years and still fall away. Strong established companies might last a hundred years yet still fail. It is only the individual that has a future and whatever that may be is up *to* the individual. The only security someone has is in their soul and that security is found in the belief in yourself whenever you meet an adversity or a crisis that knocks you back. A security in the hunger and desire to create meaning in your life. Having the security to leave your mark. Having the security to be yourself.

> True security lies within you. It
> enables you to successfully overcome
> overwhelming challenges.

'How laughable it is to me now to think that I could ever be insecure by following my heart! How embarrassing to think that I have been so foolish in days past to look for my inner security outside of me!'

Feeling the strength flow back into him, Chris raised himself from his resting-place and continued once more.

A short time later he could see that the path ahead of him would lead him into another valley, which was deeper and indeed seemed darker than the one he was crossing. As he approached, he noticed two figures following a path that skirted around this darker valley. When the first of them, whose name was Liquidate, arrived at where the path joined with Chris's he noticed our pilgrim and waited for him.

'You don't want to think about going down there,' he said.

'Why ever not?' asked Chris.

'Because it is the Valley of the Dark Night of the Soul,' said the other, named Bankrupt, who had now caught up. 'It is said that few who enter are ever able to get through.'

'But it looks as if you have both just passed through,' said Chris.

'We haven't actually gone through the middle of it,' said Bankrupt. 'We had each been skirting the edge of it, trying to find a way through, when we met up with each other.'

'Mind you,' added Liquidate, 'just doing that has been a dreadful experience in itself.'

'Though you must admit that we have both grown from the experience,' said Bankrupt. 'And if we hadn't both been trying to get through we would not have met up with each other, which has not made us feel so alone as we did before, has it?'

'It is true that a person will feel less alone when meeting another who has travelled the same path,' said Chris. 'But tell me where have you come from and where are you going.'

'Yes, and well you might ask,' began Liquidate. 'For I have

come a long way and, it would seem, I still have some way to go. That's if I can ever get out of this infernal Valley of Embarrassment.

'I'm originally from Façade Town in State Ploy. I had a company selling financial services. It's what made our town what it was, but what none of us fully realised was that everyone was in the same business. We were all selling services, but there were no real products being manufactured. It came to the point that everyone could only sell futures, for nothing really existed.

'However,' Liquidate continued, 'borrowing was easy and following the philosophy that if you could act the part, you would get more business, we borrowed more. That way we could buy all the trappings of success and, of course, market ourselves more. Anyway, initially the business went from strength to strength, well, at least we thought it did. We were seen at all the right places with all the right people and the media started writing about us as *the* company to watch. Perhaps in hindsight we unwittingly believed our own propaganda because, before we realised it, we were way overextended. And by that time it was too late and we had to close the company. I'm now on my way to the New Settlement in the State of Limbo to see what advice I can get from the Administrators there.'

'Perhaps it would be better if you by-passed there and set off towards Service City,' suggested Chris.

'But I don't need to go there, as there is nothing about service that I am seeking to learn,' replied Liquidate. 'Indeed, there is no industry that understands better than ours what good service is. No, what I need is to be able to start again so that I can win back the respect of my peers. It's so embarrassing not having the trappings of success I used to have.'

'Well, at least you kept your home,' said Bankrupt. 'At least you didn't lose all your personal money. You just lost your company. No doubt creditors lost out more than you did. I lost everything! Listening to you makes me wonder that, just because we found ourselves on the same road, we are perhaps not such kindred spirits as I first hoped.'

'Maybe by skirting the Valley that lies before us, you are not facing what you really should be facing about yourself,' offered Chris. 'Possibly you may benefit from passing through it.'

'There's no way that I'm ready to pass through there,' replied Liquidate, 'and I don't see why I should have to anyway. It may be that creditors lost more than I did, but at least their good name didn't suffer, as mine has. Anyway that was a risk they took, after all they only invested in me because they thought they were on to a good thing!'

'They more than likely invested in you because they believed in you,' said Chris. 'But either way they were still, in effect, your customers. You had a duty to serve them to the best of your ability. It strikes me that you used their investment to serve your own ends.'

'Who are you to judge me?' shouted Liquidate. 'It strikes me that from the look of you, you've been fighting your own battle and one of your own making, no doubt. We know all about such things in State Ploy, you know.'

'I wasn't in the least bit judging you,' said Chris calmly. 'I was looking at your story from my own point of view. Your story indicates to me that you believe your predicament is not your fault.'

'It isn't! And it's therefore grossly unfair that this has happened,' said Liquidate.

'Yet, in business we must recognise who our customers are, and we must make it our personal responsibility to serve them as much through choice, as duty,' said Chris. 'The investors and shareholders of your company were as much customers as those clients were that you advised on their finances. Both provided money in return for the service that you must have promised them. Otherwise why would they do such a thing?'

'They did so because the *company* promised them, not I,' said Liquidate.

'But you were the company. You formed it so it was merely an extension of you,' said Chris. 'Taking personal responsibility is not about hiding behind legal documents. Since when can a legal document take the place of integrity? You must ask yourself why you went into business. Was it to make money out of your clients, or for your clients? Was it for the accolade of what being in business would bring you, or for the benefits that you could bring to others because of it?'

'Look, I just did what everybody does and unluckily it didn't work out for me,' said Liquidate. 'But I'm going to make sure I have a stronger base next time. Now, if you'll both excuse me, I must make my way to New Settlement.'

As Liquidate got up to leave, Chris said, 'If you insist on going the way I have just come I strongly urge you to make your way directly out of this valley, for at the top you will find Integrity House.'

'Thank you, but I'm bound for the State of Limbo before I do anything else,' replied Liquidate.

'Then if that's the case you may discover that you chance upon two people that suit you anyway,' offered Chris. 'Both are from that State and one of them is always keen to provide a pass to get you there.'

It is our personal responsibility to recognise who our customers are and to serve them by choice and not duty alone.

As he watched his former travelling companion leave, Bankrupt said, 'Perhaps because of my current despair I latched on to someone who made me feel as though I wasn't alone in my predicament.'

'It is natural to seek either motivation or solace in people we believe to be like-minded individuals,' said Chris. 'But whenever we are vulnerable we must be careful about what we think we need. What we perceive to be like-minded behaviours and attitudes that fit in with our individual preferences and desires, can in reality turn out to be a complete anathema to us.'

'You know, there were a couple of occasions when I was strongly inclined to enter into the valley below,' said Bankrupt. 'Then, when I met with my recent companion, I became less inclined to enter.'

'It is better to follow our strong inclinations than passively submit to the environment that surrounds us,' said Chris. 'But tell me what's your tale? How did you come to be here in the first place?'

'I am from the Zone of Enterprise not far from here,' began Bankrupt. 'Though I did have a goal to visit Service City, my overriding goal was to get started in business on my own account. Then, when I had made it, I was going to visit there in style. But I always believed in the stories that I'd heard from people who had already been there.'

'What stories?' asked Chris inquisitively.

'That the secret to winning and keeping customers is to reward them,' said Bankrupt. 'And that the most important customer to win over is yourself, because the best salesperson is the true believer.'

'If you have been fortunate to learn such things, how did you come to lose everything?' asked Chris.

'Well, perhaps it was because a little knowledge is a dangerous thing or because to know and not to do is still not to know,' replied Bankrupt. 'Although, if I'm honest, someone told me that only *after* I had lost everything. The point was, though, that I did believe in the products that I was selling. At first things went brilliantly, but as my success grew, for some reason I began to imagine that it couldn't last. I then started to lose my earlier confidence in winning sales. Then I began to worry about the competition. There was so much of it, you know. It's odd because I'd never been aware of how much when I first started out.

'Then I began to think that my prices might be too high. So I decided to make my products the cheapest available. That seemed to do the trick at first because, with all focus on sales, we sold loads of products. Of course, we weren't able to provide the same after-sales service, but that didn't seem to matter because we could hardly keep up with the demand as it was. Then they stopped selling again. So I reduced the prices again, but still they wouldn't sell. I thought it was because the market was saturated; but another competitor's products, which were all but identical to mine, were still selling well and at a *higher* price!

'It became so desperate that I had to put *everything* I had into just keeping going, but the more I pushed customers as to the attraction of what they were buying, the less they wanted to know.' Eventually, I had to close down, hardly got anything for all the stock I was left with and well, you know the rest.'

'Where are you heading now?' asked Chris.

'Well nowhere really. Since my world fell apart I've been stuck in this valley,' Bankrupt said as he motioned around him. Then pointing at the darkness below him added, 'And I've already told you that there's been a couple of times when I've wandered into that dark valley below. But the first time I came quickly out because I felt an immense fear of failure to get through to the other side. And the second time I did the same because I felt an overwhelming fear of success if I did get through.'

'I said earlier,' consoled Chris, 'that sometimes we must go where our leaning takes us, as it is the best way for each of us to grow. Such paths require us to address elements in ourselves that are not supportive, even though we mistakenly believe they are. Because I am not as close to what has happened to you as you are, I see things differently. It is clear to me that even though your fear of success was groundless, you allowed it to fuel insecurity in your original belief about what you were doing. With your original conviction overruled, you then rationalised that you must act differently in order not to lose what you had gained. This fuelled the fear of failure, another baseless insecurity. Both these fears worked against you successfully. Only by passing through that valley below, will you be able to face such fears and in doing so defeat them.'

Fear of succeeding or fear of failing both affect your inner belief in your ability to accomplish something and see it through. They make you doubt your ability to cope if things don't turn out as you had hoped. Trust in your convictions and you will overcome this fear.

'But who wants to go through the Dark Night of the Soul?' said Bankrupt. 'Look at it, the wood is so thick in that valley down there that you can hardly see the trees. Even if a person were to enter, how would they ever be sure about coming out the other side?'

'The path must go through the wood because you can see how this one and several others lead right up to it,' said Chris.

'Then why don't we pass through it together, side by side?' suggested Bankrupt.

'Well, for one thing the path doesn't look wide enough for even one person to pass by, let alone for two to go side by side,' said Chris. 'And for another thing I don't believe that our paths are one and the same.'

'What do you mean by that?' enquired Bankrupt.

'Simply that I am confident about where I am heading, whereas you are still recovering from where you are coming from,' replied Chris.

'But you just said that the best thing for me was to pass through that valley?' said Bankrupt.

'Yes, because I fervently believe that you must face your fears, but you cannot do that with me. Nor can I with you. It is something we must each face alone. Entering together will only cause us to rely on each other and in doing so we would only be borrowing the strength of the other. We must take the opportunity to build our own strength of character by passing through it in our own way, taking our own path. It is not wise to rely too much on the strength of another, as we may not always be with another in times of difficulty.'

'Well, if you forgive me,' said Bankrupt quietly, 'I'll rest here a little while longer first. What you say is right, it's just that you look so prepared and confident.'

'Because of your recent experiences you are probably better prepared than I,' replied Chris. 'Indeed, having lost everything as you have, you are in a stronger position than I. You have everything to gain. The path ahead may well be the kindred spirit you require right now, helping you to emerge with confidence in yourself once more. The path may even be one that you could not have taken were it not for your experiences. As for my part, I am not certain what I must face for I have not lost everything as you have.'

'Maybe not, but I get the feeling that you have been prepared to give up everything for what you believe in,' said Bankrupt.

'That may be one reason why our paths are different,' replied Chris. 'But I won't say adieu for it may be that our paths cross again. In the meantime, I will give to you my Shield of Sequence. It has served its purpose for me, having given me the discipline to take one step at a time. Look upon what you have gone through as just one sequential step on your path to success. You have no need of my Sword of Steadfastness for it is clear to me that you already have what it offers in abundance.'

Bankrupt was moved by the gesture. 'Thank you,' he said. 'You know, when you refused my company a moment ago I resented you. Now that you have explained your reasons I realise that in refusing me you were actually giving me a greater service: the opportunity to stand on my own two feet. I will not forget your words of support nor your gift. So thank you again and may you fare well on your own journey.'

On approaching the Valley of the Dark Night of the Soul, Chris felt an awful sense of foreboding. 'It is so dark and much more overgrown than I thought. Perhaps there is a way around it after all? But what am I saying? That I want to spend for ever skirting around here! Anyway, it cannot be worse than my meeting with Securi-I-tas, can it?'

Chris continued to talk to himself for confidence and as he did so he thought he could hear other voices. 'Perhaps it's a fellow traveller also talking to himself?'

As he continued, the valley became so dark that it became almost impossible to see the path ahead and he had to feel his way with his own Mettle Gauntlets, which were now so much a part of him. With his vision unclear it appeared to Chris that his other senses were becoming more acute. On his hands and knees he felt for the ruts and pitfalls that randomly lay in his path. The voices he had heard seemed now to whisper persuasively in his ear.

'There's no point in biting off more than you can chew, you know?' said one. 'Give up on your empty pilgrimage. You must realise that you're chasing rainbows,' laughed another, 'there's no such thing as good service. It's a pipe dream.' 'You're wasting your time with all this touchy-feely stuff,' sneered another, 'it doesn't work. You should be getting on with your job and stop wasting everyone's time.' 'And fancy leaving your family on their own!' criticised one, 'what sort of a person does that? Some responsibility that it is, letting them fend for themselves.'

Such was the incessant tormenting that Chris couldn't stop himself from arguing back in defence. And the more he did so, the stronger the arguments he heard became.

'But I have to do this!' protested Chris. 'If a man doesn't follow what is important to him, what has he got?'

'Well, whatever he may have, he's going to lose,' a voice sneered. 'Why should anyone want to stay around someone who's so selfish? No one likes people who are only out for themselves, hiding behind some noble cause.'

'I'm not out for myself,' argued Chris, 'though I believe my cause is noble. I stand to deliver and I'm determined to discover the secrets of doing so.'

'Stop fooling yourself, *please!*' an exasperated voice sighed. 'Why don't you just simply know your place? You have a fine home and a good job, all this rocking the boat isn't going to do you any good at all.'

For what seemed an eternity, Chris argued with the voices and got angrier and angrier. The voices kept up their barrage, sometimes persuasive, sometimes sneering and always patronising. In his blind anger Chris tripped into a particularly deep pit. Clasping on to the edge his legs swung in an empty void, while the voices that were now all around him laughed. With his life now at risk, his focus changed and he ignored the continual taunting of the voices suggesting that he just let go and give up the fight. 'There's no way I'm going to get stuck in this rut,' he shouted. His mettle held good and he slowly pulled himself up and out of danger.

'You see what happens when you do things that are beyond you,' said a voice quietly. 'At least you've had a go, now just accept that where you're hoping to go is not for the likes of you. Go back now, no one will be any the wiser. Otherwise you'll only fall again and what if you can't get out? Then what will you do?'

'Even though the way ahead is dark I can see what you are all about,' said Chris, realising that until now he had been fighting fire with fire. 'Do you think that I don't know who you are?'

'We only have your interests at heart you know,' answered a voice. 'Yes, we're only trying to protect you from yourself,' said another. 'It's better to know your place, really it is, for what good would it do if everyone went around doing their own thing?' said another.

'Thank you for your well meaning admonitions and cautionary advice,' said Chris. 'But please forgive me if I choose not to take it and indeed no longer even listen. For I realise *now* that there are many voices within us, but only one *true* one. You voices have no right to be here because you all belong to the *past*. I hold no malice towards you and indeed forgive you, for I accept the responsibility for your existence. Because, however dormant you have been I have always kept you alive and given you any power you may have. Many of you I now recognise from my formative years when your admonishments were considered to be an assistance to my development.

'I now admit to myself that I was simply duplicating what had been said to me when I was young. Echoes of words intended to control, rather than direct, spoken to me in childhood. Even though there have been times that I vowed to myself that I would never repeat what had been said to me, I confess there were days when I would catch myself saying them.

'Conditioning is so duplicable that is it any wonder the "sins of the father" carry through generation after generation? I now understand what Intuition was telling me when he said that there is no better soul to direct me than that of my own. With so many voices within us giving us conflicting advice, no wonder it is nearly impossible to have unity within our mind. Yet, if people are to be truly themselves they must attain unity within. For it is only with such inner unity that each of us can become the true conduit we are intended to be. The special spiritual conduit that connects us with the very source of Creation that unifies us all.

'Such a conduit provides us with our creativity, our innovation and our own special purpose for us to fulfil. A conduit through which each of us can receive all we ever need in the form of comfort, solace, hope, determination, imagination and consideration. And you have all shown me how to open this conduit. It is to filter out those sounds that do not resonate in harmony within me. It is to go deep into myself and feel the musical words that come to me and strike a chord of rightness. And what is the best way to do that? Why, simply to talk to myself calmly and not in anger or fear. For I can confirm better how I really think about something when I hear myself repeat whatever it is out loud.

Unity of thought will make you strong in hope, determination and imagination and prevent doubt. Through this unity you are able to lose the questioning voices and trust in your own true convictions.

'Listening to your voices and allowing you to get to me almost destroyed me. Now is it clear to me that I must positively affirm to myself what I am about, whenever I am uncertain or fearful. Your cautionary warnings to me that previously caused me to so deeply doubt myself have simply proved that affirmations work. I will now harness their power for my benefit, not my ill. Through positive self-talk I will affirm to myself what is important to me and I will affirm what I want to achieve. So, go away negative inner voices, your days are at an end.'

At those words Chris could at last see light at the end of the tunnelled path ahead of him. Within a few moments he was once more out in the open, this time standing in the bright rays of the morning sun. He realised that he had spent the whole night being subjected to the horrors of the dark valley.

> We can be the person we are intended to become, when we attain true unity within ourselves.

After a short time Chris came to the top of ridge where he was able to survey the land for some way before him. Not too far away there was a solitary figure on the same path as Chris who seemed to be heading in the same direction. Our pilgrim quickened his pace and nearing the fellow traveller felt certain that he knew him.

'Hey, hold up and wait for me!' shouted Chris when he had caught up enough to be in earshot.

Self-Reliance turned, stopped and waited for Chris to join him.

'I thought it was you,' said Chris, a little breathless. 'I learned that you were on the same road as I and was hoping to catch up with you.'

'Well it's good to see you again, friend,' replied Self-Reliance. 'It's quite a few years since we last walked side by side, you know.'

'Yes, we certainly seemed to enjoy more freedom when we

were young,' said Chris, 'since then there was always some place I had to go, but I always thought I would meet up with you again.'

'And on the same road it would appear,' said Self-Reliance.

'Are you going to the Land of Prosperity and Service City?' asked Chris.

'Ah, I know well the Land of Prosperity and have been fortunate to pass through it many times. But I have never been to Service City, yet I am heading towards there now and it is partly because of you,' said Self-Reliance.

'Me,' said Chris surprised. 'How?'

'Well, I had heard of Service City, but had never really had the inclination to go there before. Until recently that is when I discovered I had left the Land of Prosperity and wandered back into your world of Mediocrity and decided to visit you.'

'I never knew, why didn't you tell me?'

'Because you had already left on your "business holiday", as Christine put it. She told me that you had this hankering to seek out some enlightened service and change your world.'

'How was she?' asked Chris.

'She was fine. She said it was better to have you away following your dream rather than at home being frustrated about everything. Anyway, she told me that you had been determined to leave the City of Apathy and visit Service City. This got me thinking. Although I have always believed that I could do whatever I could through my own self-sufficiency, perhaps my nature of going it alone for so long at a time does not help me. I wondered what you felt that I didn't? Then it came to me. If I sought out the same place it would take me to the destination that my firmness of direction was unable to and could therefore provide the key for me to stay in the Land of Prosperity.'

'Which way did you leave?' asked Chris. 'Via Change Border?'

'Well, first I met a man who was a colleague of yours, though I must say he was pretty derisive about you. He apparently left you at the Pub of Procrastination drowning your frustration, he said.'

'That was Indecisive!' said Chris. 'It was he who suggested that we rest at that awful place, though now I accept that it was fully my responsibility. But he didn't direct you there did he?'

'Well, he directed me to the pub but I could see that he wasn't a man who was sure of his word. Why, he acted as if he couldn't even trust himself. And the bitterness he exuded for having been excited about leaving Apathy with you, then not doing so, was plain to see. It was clear that he blames you for making him look a fool, though I think he has quite easily done that for himself through his own mouth.

'So, I made my way out of the city past the Pub of Procrastination and came to Change Border. From there I was directed to take the Road of Independence, which suited me well, and I arrived directly at a large Hill.'

You have stronger command over your life when you remain unconcerned about outcomes.

'Then your road took you beyond Accountability's house,' said Chris. 'That is how you overtook me on the road, for I stayed there several days.'

'That must be the case, though where we meet now seems apt,' replied Self-Reliance.

'Yes, the right place and at the right time!' said Chris, 'just how I was advised it would be when you stick to the right path.'

'At the bottom of the Hill I met with two called Arrogance and Pride. They asked where I was heading and I told them.

Both of them tried to persuade me to join them saying that they knew of a shortcut, which went directly to Service City. I told them that I was very sure about how I wanted to get there and my motives included joining an old friend along the way.'

'That's why your path took you in a different direction to mine,' said Chris. 'You had firmness of motive already.'

'Of course, though I was hard put to by those rogues,' answered Self-Reliance. 'They told me that a person like me was his own man and did not have to follow such motives or a course that involved another. I thanked them for their compliment adding that I would now be on my way. Well they didn't seem to like the idea of me leaving. Pride seemed hurt and said that for me to go when there was so much more to discuss was offensive. Arrogance just turned nasty saying that I was lucky to have met up with them in the first place and how dare I turn down their offer of a shortcut.'

'What happened?' said Chris with concern.

'Well, I knew that I would have to get away from their influence as quickly as possible for it was obvious that they were out to capture innocent travellers to put down with their whims and vagary of shortcuts. So I made a dash for it up the Hill. They must have expected it for they chased after me shouting for me to do as I was told if I knew what was good for me. Anyway, they got in the way of each other and were unable to catch me.

'Soon after that, I passed a pleasant spot and I was about to take a rest when I saw two people, a couple I think. Anyway, as it looked as though they were having a difference of opinion, and hadn't seen me, I thought it would be better to go on. Later, when I did rest, I looked back down at them. I could see that the woman was making her way back down the Hill, while the man was busy making himself a drink.'

'Coffee, no doubt,' put in Chris. 'That'll have been Habit

and his girlfriend Curious, for certain. I never met her but I did talk with him and you were wise not to stop. As for me, I fell asleep there and was careless enough to lose my charter. But tell me, was the view good from the top because it was dark when I reached it?'

'Well, actually there was not a great to deal to see because the summit was covered in cloud,' replied Self-Reliance. 'Mind you,' he added with amusement, 'it's not often I have my head in the clouds so it was a new experience! But more seriously though, because I couldn't see ahead to my destination, I had the most overwhelming reluctance to continue on my travels. I felt as if I should just go back down and forget my recently forged quest.'

'Then I was lucky to reach the top at night after all,' said Chris. 'Though I was not so fortunate as to miss meeting Criticism and Suspicion and a couple of other scoundrels on the road at night.'

'I met with no other person until I entered the first of the two valleys behind us,' said Self-Reliance quietly. 'Though I wish I had not, for Providence did not much come to my aid.'

'Did you meet with that fiend Securi-I-tas?' questioned Chris taking the opportunity to briefly share his own dreadful experience.

'It is good that you defeated such a monster,' said Self-Reliance. 'For my part, I had no occasion to meet with such a manifestation, but I did meet with Hostility and Spite. When I met them on the road I hailed them in a hearty manner as befits fellow travellers, but my friendly manner did not go down at all well.

'"What gives you the right to be so confident and courteous?" Hostility said to me. "Coming down into our valley with your airs and graces as if you own the place! We don't want none of your sort here, be off with you."

127

'Well I was not going to be put off my course just because of some unfriendly words,' continued Self-Reliance. 'So I told him that this was the direction I was heading, that I was sorry if I had inadvertently offended him and that perhaps he could put me right on where I had gone wrong. His friend Spite whispered something in his companion's ear, which seemed to mollify him because he became friendlier and went to one side to let me pass. As I did so they both tripped me up and were upon me before I could get up.

'It was plain to me then that Spite had suggested it, but by then it was almost too late to defend myself, so I curled up in to a ball and protected myself as best I could from their blows. Eventually they gave up and ran off with Hostility laughing and his friend Spite shouting, "That'll teach you for thinking you're better than we are!"'

'How terrible!' said Chris. 'But why did they do such a thing?'

'Because *they* believed that my manner threatened their security, and people attack what they perceive as threatening,' said Self-Reliance.

'And what people perceive they allow to distort their beliefs, values and in turn their communications with others, of course,' offered Chris.

'Yes, and the fact that people are not aware of the basis of their values and beliefs, which only makes them feel more threatened when someone appears to be different to the way they are. They feel insecure and don't know why,' said Self-Reliance.

We are all individuals and see things from
a unique perspective. This perspective can
convince us wrongly that what someone else
is doing is going to threaten our own security,

so we feel it necessary to attack them to defend ourselves.

'I remember at school,' said Chris, 'there was always a crowd that used to enjoy poking fun at someone if that person was good at a particular subject. They even picked on me once just because I got the highest mark in the class a couple of times in a row. They accused me of being a swot and trying to show them up.' Chris paused for a moment while he reflected on the emotions the crowd had made him feel at the time. He thought of his own children who attended the same school as he had done. 'I wonder what the schools are like in Service City?'

'Well, from what I have heard about the emphasis on learning and consideration,' replied Self-Reliance, 'I can only believe that each pupil develops their inherent empathy, thoughtfulness and motivation to the full.'

'And I bet they're praised for their strengths instead of being rebuked for their weaknesses, and are taught how to be the best they can be rather than to get by how they can,' said Chris. 'Yes, I would like to send my children to a school like that.'

'One day all schools will be like that, though it may take a few generations,' said Self-Reliance. 'And I truly believe it will happen, for the ripples of such schooling already exist. I have seen them in my travels.'

'Tell me,' said Chris, 'did you meet with anyone else in the Valley of Embarrassment?'

'Yes, I met with Disappointment,' said his companion. 'His discourse was painful to bear, for after telling me the story of his sad life, he started on me. He told me it must have been a setback for me too not to be able to stay in one place for long. He asked me if I could imagine the chagrin that I must have caused my parents for always wanting to do my own thing. How calamity must have followed me throughout my life. That with the way

I was going I could only ever expect hardship, misadventure and desolation.

'To say I felt crushed was an understatement,' continued Self-Reliance. Meeting with him gave me a sense of foreboding that I had not experienced before. But I was able to keep my wits about me and asked him why he didn't think about how he could be beneficial to others. He seemed pleased that I had asked such a question and indeed told me that people seldom asked him such a thing. "People don't generally like me," he said to me, "why, some will even cross the street to get away from me if they see me coming. Yet, if they took the time to just greet me and even asked how I came to be there, before they passed me by, as you have done, they would see that I am not so bad after all."'

'Sort of meet him head on?' asked Chris.

'I believe that is what he was trying to say,' said Self-Reliance. 'But you must admit, I said to him, that you do have a tendency to make people feel somewhat morose.'

'What did he say to that?' asked Chris.

'Well, it was odd because he told me that it wasn't *him* that made people melancholy. They did that to themselves simply because they weren't prepared to meet him face to face. He said their thoughts drew him towards them and then, when he appeared, to give them some guidance, they ran away from him. And with that he passed me by.'

'Reflecting on what he had said, I realised we have two choices in life. One is to remain happy whatever the outcome; and the other is to only be happy if the outcome is what we hoped for.'

Choose either to be happy no matter what the outcome of your decisions or choose only to be happy if everything goes to plan. The

choice that gives you the most control over your life is obviously the first.

'Well, certainly, the first choice is the most obvious one,' said Chris.

'Of course, but almost all of us continue to choose the second; yet by remaining unconcerned about our outcomes, as the first choice involves, we put ourselves in stronger command of our lives. And how could we better serve ourselves than having greater command over ourselves?'

'Which brings meaning to the principle of serving yourself first before serving others, for it is the best way to serve others!' said Chris. 'Serving yourself doesn't mean *taking* first, it simply means putting oneself in order first!'

'Which you can only do when you have command over yourself. Doing unto others as we would have them do unto us is fine so long as we learn to serve ourselves as the very special beings we are. But the reality is that people *treat* others the way they treat themselves, though they are seldom aware of it. The energy, for instance, that each of us employs in self-hurt, is the same energy that we use to hurt others. When we meet with a setback, our tendency is to want to take it out on others.'

'Then it seems to me, said Chris, 'that it is important for us each to learn how to overcome setback and rejection. Because it is not possible to be of service to others without such understanding.'

'Which means we must constantly seek to extend ourselves,' said Self-Reliance. 'For in doing so, we bring about the greatest possible value that we can feel about ourselves as well as what we bring to others. For in truth it's not what we achieve, it's what we become.'

'Look!' said Chris, 'We've reached the ridge! At last we can leave these valleys behind us.'

To Be a Pilgrim ...

- Do not seek your inner security in the opinion of others
- Self-respect and integrity are the only security you'll ever need
- Do not passively become a product of your environment — retain your unique sense of identity
- Regularly affirm what is important to you and what you want to achieve
- Follow the order of *being*, before *doing*, and *doing* before *having*
- What you achieve will be proportionate to your desire for it
- Accept full responsibility for whatever happens to you
- Know where you are going so that you can recognise it when you get there

Chapter Five

Passing through Superficial Town

Chris and Self-Reliance stood at the top of the ridge and gazed at the path ahead of them. In the distance they could just make out buildings.

'It's good to see you both again,' said a voice, 'and travelling together this time. I knew that you would meet up.'

Turning to their side they each recognised the guide who had directed them to Change Border.

'Intuition!' said Chris. 'Well, it's good to bump into you again. I was just wondering what lay ahead.'

'I can tell you that whatever it is you will view it differently than you used to,' replied their friend. 'For I see that you have shed the burden that so weighed you down before. Indeed it is clear that you now carry an air of conviction and self-belief in its place which tells me that you have emerged victorious in the battle of self-improvement.'

'It is because I understand that self-improvement is a duty,' said Chris. 'The responsibility that each of us owe to ourselves as members of society. We serve society better through our aspirations rather than our frustrations. And to be the best we can be is the best way we can serve.'

'Well said! However, you will soon be entering a sancti-monious place that will not appreciate such a philosophy,' said Intuition. 'You must proceed with care through Superficial

Town, for that is the name of the place. For its Pretension Market beguiles travellers with false offers and has waylaid many fine pilgrims before you.'

> Your hopes, dreams, desires, goals and ambitions are the things that will make the world a better, more loving and positive place for you and everyone around you – not your frustrations, which will make you feel only resentment for people and the life you lead.

'How can such a place exist on the road to the Ground of Good Fortune?' asked Self-Reliance. 'I must say I have not heard of the place before.'

'That's because you have never sought Service City before now,' replied Intuition. 'You may find it hard to imagine but there was a time, long forgotten now, when this road was incredibly busy. Full of people heading for the Ground of Good Fortune. Superficial Town came into existence to meet the increasing demands of travellers who sought sustenance on their journey there and were not prepared to wait for the rewards at the end of the road. The town grew quickly as people were deceived into thinking that living there was much better than continuing on their journey. Rumours became rife that to go on meant sacrificing everything for nothing. These false stories were started by some self-interested individuals of which Judge Find-Fault was the most influential. Pilgrims were offered vanities in the form of titles, honours, lands, possessions and pleasures in return for abandoning their dreams and staying.

'It suited some people to stay because, though they knew what they wanted, they had never really been prepared to pay the price to get it. Now, of course, the same people do not like it when others appear committed to going where they themselves were unable. To allow such a person to pass would highlight their own inadequacies, so they try to prevent it by the same means that prevented them, Pretension Market.'

'Must we go by that way?' enquired Chris. 'Surely, there must be another route?'

'I wish there were but at this point in your journey there is only one path before entering the Ground of Good Fortune. It's as if all roads meet at this junction,' replied Intuition.

'Have you any advice we should follow before entering this town?' asked Self-Reliance.

'My advice to you both has consistently been to be yourself, above all else. You now have a clearer idea, of course, of who you are, where you are going and how to be yourself. But I have to tell you that because you now both exude what you are about, the townspeople will instantly pick you out as not being one of them. They will see you as someone to be persuaded to stay, or be destroyed.'

'Destroyed?' said Chris

'Unfortunately, your presence may completely conflict with what they have deluded themselves that they stand for,' answered Intuition. 'They will, therefore, question you about your beliefs and your inevitable replies will be viewed as a slight against the way they live.'

'But we would never want to put another down,' argued Chris. 'So perhaps if we just keep to ourselves and pass through they might leave us alone.'

'Whatever you are able to do to get through, you must do in line with your values,' said Intuition. 'Just remember to keep your mind always on why you want to get through. You have already met and defeated Securi-I-tas by keeping your resolve, haven't you?'

'Yes, indeed I have, though I was tested to the point of breaking,' said Chris. 'And on that matter, could you tell me why it seemed that the more I fought, the stronger Securi-I-tas seemed to get?'

Follow things through by protecting your resolve to do so. Customer loyalty is built on follow-through. The right time to follow through, coupled with the determination to do so is a major factor in all achievement.

'Because the monster drew its strength from *your* fear, *your* doubts and *your* insecurities,' answered Intuition. 'It wasn't until you decided never to give up, no matter what it cost you, that the creature's rule over you was at an end. Nothing can resist the will of someone that is prepared to stake his or her existence on accomplishing what they have set out to fulfil.'

'The interesting thing was that the instant before I overcame Securi-I-tas I knew that I would,' said Chris. 'It was as though I saw the outcome in my mind's-eye and my action just automatically followed through.'

'I think I know what you're saying,' said Self-Reliance. 'It's that sense of command that comes to you just at the precise moment when you are about to do something that scares you, yet excites you and that you *feel* you can do. And if you don't do it then the moment passes and you are not able to do it. Like parachuting out of an aeroplane the first time or diving off a board into a swimming pool, or saying something you believe to be right, when all others stay quiet.'

'There is truth in the old adage of striking while the iron is hot,' said Intuition. 'Too hot and the steel is too malleable, too cold and the steel is brittle. To get the finest cutting edge the blacksmith must strike just at the right time.'

'It's as if an unmistakable sense of determined will-power,

built up inside you, co-ordinates all your belief,' said Chris. 'At that moment you must follow through, or be lost.'

'I have learned that the timing of doing something coupled with a determined follow-through is a major factor in all achievement,' said Self-Reliance.

'It is true that so many fine ideals, dreams and goals have been lost for ever simply because they have not been followed through,' said Intuition. 'The same applies even more so with relationships. The lack of saying something when it should be said, or the *not* saying something when it shouldn't be said are damaging enough. But by far the main reason why relationships do not grow and strengthen, as they should, is because of lack of follow-through. When people say something and do not follow it through it is as bad as promising and then not delivering. There should be no need to promise in a relationship, for relationship building is about trust investment. How can you expect to build a relationship when you excuse yourself for not doing what you said you would?'

'I believe that marketing is not about selling, it's about building relationships,' said Chris. 'And, in all honesty, the principle of trust investment is as applicable in a family relationship as much as it is in any other relationship. Saying to my family that I'll do something and then not doing it is no different to saying to a customer I'll phone you back and then not doing so. Whether one is family or not isn't the point. I would have raised the hopes of both and not followed through.'

'And then my old friend Rationale,' said Intuition, 'would first defend your actions with your family by telling you that they'll understand and forgive you because you have to work. Then, he would defend your actions with the customer suggesting that it's only a customer and they won't mind because no one ever phones back when they say they will anyway. But, in truth, however imperceptible it may be, both relationships are weakened.'

'Trust is created by demonstrating dependability, responsibility and by maximum communication,' put in Self-Reliance. 'Suppose a client phones and asks you to leave a message with the person who handles his account. You pass on the message but if you then phone back the client to confirm that the message was received he, or she, will know that the communication has been completed. This follow-through service is generally not expected and rarely performed, but is tremendously appreciated. It's no different to asking someone to change an appointment for you and then that person confirming that they have done so on your behalf. It may not seem worth the bother, but it can make a business reputation or break it. It is the small considerate acts that reassure people and help to build trust. For they develop people's confidence in you and help build your reputation as someone who is competent and trustworthy.'

'Close attention to such relationship details will determine the way a person is regarded,' said Intuition. 'The person who takes on complex tasks and has no time for the mundane details overlooks an essential aspect of business. For, in truth, it is the ordinary, inglorious tasks that are so important to relationship building and are the best route for a successful career.'

> Follow-through service is greatly appreciated
> because it is rarely performed and unexpected.
> A customer will trust your ability to provide
> future good service as they will not have often
> received treatment like this before.

'To hear this is disheartening; where I come from there is only reliance on voice-mail, electronic prepared answers to customers' queries. And our call centres are so busy they forget to do what they may have told one of their numerous callers, because the next call immediately follows,' said Chris. 'And they know if they don't get around to sorting out a query that it doesn't really matter because the customer will simply call back again anyway.'

'You're right! As a student I worked in one of those call centres and the only training I got was during the first day on how many calls to take,' said Self-Reliance. 'And the only qualification required was that I spoke well at the interview. I had to take calls all day long and most of the time I just had to appease the customer, because there was little else I could do. If we couldn't help them we were told to say the computers were down and could they call back. Most of the calls were to mollify the caller for not being able to deliver what a particular advertisement offered. Some people stayed on the phone for ages just to hear that the information they had been given, which had made them phone in the first place, was not exactly right. You can imagine they were pretty annoyed at being misled and having their time wasted.'

'It's amazing to think that two per cent of the *working* population are now employed in call centres,' said Chris. 'That's more people than the massive coal mining industry employed at its peak!'

'When you reach Service City you will learn how the principles of Enlightened Service always follow through on the customer's behalf,' said Intuition. 'These principles may well seem ahead of their time but the fact is that they are timeless and will never change. With all manners of communication and technology being developed in business today, the pace of change seems astounding to us now. But then what we think of as progress, from a contemporary point of view, will be archaic in a hundred years. Our descendants will look at our "revolutionary" and "state-of-the-art" technology and smile at how unsophisticated it is. That is the nature of technological progress in human civilisation. But the Principles of Service that effectively share such progress for the benefit of Mankind will always remain the same.'

Intuition paused as he looked ahead of him. 'The time has come for me to now leave you again,' he said. 'Good luck and remember what we have discussed.'

Both Chris and his companion were amazed at how busy the town was that they now entered. The whole centre was one huge shopping mall with people bustling in and out of specialist shops that all promised something special.

'What an incredible array of merchandise,' said Chris, 'and look at how many people are in the shops. I wonder what the service is like inside them?'

'We should keep going straight through,' said Self-Reliance, concerned at some of the looks they were being given. 'It's better that we get on.'

'What's your hurry?' said a street trader whose name was Manipulate. 'I can see that this is your first time here yet you do not seem interested in looking at our town. Why is that, then? I'm sure it's because you don't realise what we have on offer here. Come, let me show you.'

Before our two pilgrims could protest Manipulate had led them into a large store. 'In here,' he said to them, 'we have all forms of status on offer. Take your time and look around. You're sure to see something you want.'

Chris watched as all the assistants eyed him expectantly. Several of the younger ones came up to him, one after the other asking, 'Can I help you?'

'We're just looking, actually,' said Chris which elicited the reply:

'What is it you're looking for?'

'They must be on commission or something,' said Self-Reliance, 'because they won't leave us alone.'

'And look at the older assistants,' said Chris. 'They seem to be too full of their own importance to pay us any attention at all.'

'Good, while they're not looking let's get out of here, it's so hot and the music is so loud you can hardly hear yourself think, let alone talk,' said Self-Reliance.

'How can you be leaving already?' said Manipulate who had been watching them. 'Don't tell me there's nothing in here at all for you.'

'Well, we have everything we need at the moment,' replied Chris.

'Need for what?' enquired Manipulate. 'You're on your way to *somewhere* then, I take it?'

Before Self-Reliance could suggest to Chris that it would be better to keep quiet about their destination, Manipulate got it out of him that they were on the way to the Land of Prosperity and Service City.

'In that case, we have *lots* that you should be interested in!' said Manipulate on hearing this. 'You must have a fine frame for your charter that you must be carrying. A fine frame makes it much more meaningful, you know. Why, take a look at ours hanging over there. Doesn't it look good?'

Chris was taken over to read it and was shocked at how similar some of the wording was to his own, though the meaning was clearly different.

'Stand and deliver your money or your life,' it read.

In the meantime, an assistant manager called Plausible took Self-Reliance off in another direction.

'Here, come with me,' Plausible had said, 'I've got something to show you and I can assure you that you won't meet with disappointment.'

141

Then Manipulate looked at Chris and asked if our pilgrim would be good enough to share his own charter.

'I stand to deliver service for life,' said Chris.

'Then you're in luck,' said Manipulate. 'We've just the position available for you and it's a fine-sounding one, let me tell you.'

'But I'm not looking for a position,' protested Chris.

'Of course you are,' said Manipulate, 'everyone wants a good position. And this one has just come up today. Just think of the security in itself. And anyway you don't even know what it is yet. Just wait till you hear what it is. Come on we'll go and visit Prestige at the Status Department. He's always interested in seeing people who are offering something such as you.'

'But I'm not offering anything,' said Chris. 'You're offering me something, which I don't want.'

'Don't want the title *Controller* of Service Co-ordination?' said Manipulate. 'Of course you do, and I can see that you're already excited about the prospect. And the good news is that you don't really have to do anything. What more could you want? Now, what else did you want to have? What about membership to our exclusive business club? We're always looking for new blood and with me recommending you, we may even be able to see our way to getting you in as a vice-president or something. What do you think of that, eh? Now, come on, we have the whole mall to see yet. You don't want to lose out just because someone else pips you at the post for something, you know. Mind you, you should have been here last week.'

'But I wasn't here last week, so what difference would it have made anyway,' said Chris. 'And I would have missed out on the *Controller* position, which you say had *just* become available.'

'What sort of an attitude is that?' replied Manipulate. 'I'm just saying you should have been here last week! Still, at least you're here now taking the opportunity to buy.'

'But I'm not buying anything and I don't intend to buy anything either,' said Chris.

'What do you mean you're not buying anything? You've already committed yourself,' said Manipulate. 'The sign above the entrance door very clearly says that there is a minimum purchase in here.'

'Well, I'm leaving as soon as I've found my companion,' said Chris.

'Oh no you don't! You're not getting out of your obligation to purchase that easily, you know. We have a system to protect us from time wasters like you.'

Better-than-excellent customer service is never persuading or bullying someone into having something just because *you* want to move products or services. The greatest rewards come from matching the customer to the *customer's* requirements of the moment, not yours.

Meanwhile, unbeknown to Chris, Self-Reliance was being tempted by Plausible to buy a lottery ticket.

'The chances of you winning today are incredible. Just think, one quick purchase and you will be able to make all your dreams come true.'

'I'm already making my dreams come true,' said Self-Reliance, 'for every day of my life I am in command of what I want to be, do and have. And I can confidently assure you that I do not want to *have* what you are offering.'

'But how do you really *know* what you want to have until you see it?' argued Plausible. 'We're very experienced in dealing with customers, you know, and we have found that almost all buy on impulse. And we are proud to satisfy their impulse and, what's more, immediately! Where else would you get such a service? Come on, a little of what you fancy is good for you, don't you agree?'

'Yes, I do agree so long as whatever it is remains in moderation,' replied Self-Reliance. 'But that is not the point here. You are intent on selling your customers things that you convince them they need. Whatever you have a surplus of, you make into a good offer. But no matter how good a bargain may be, it is not a bargain if it is not really wanted.'

'So? Who cares? The customer doesn't seem to mind, and we certainly don't, so long as we get a sale. Now are you going to take up this offer or are you wasting my time? In which case we have a system to protect us from people like you.'

Chris and Self-Reliance were both individually arrested and met each other again when they were brought before Judge Find-Fault for examination.

'What do you think you're doing entering our peaceful town and causing a disturbance?' demanded Judge Find-Fault.

'As far as we are aware, we have not caused anything of the sort,' replied Chris. 'Moreover, our intention of passing through peacefully and quietly was prevented by your townspeople intent on selling to us.'

'And why should they not for is it not their town, their wares and therefore their right?' said Judge Find-Fault. 'I put it to you that the disturbance was caused by you *refusing* to buy, which I might add is a threat to their very livelihood and the existence of our fine town. If this was not the case why may I ask did you come here?'

'Because we are on the way to Service City and the only road to it passes through this way,' said Chris.

'And what makes you think for one moment that such a place is worth going to in preference to our fine city? Is it not true that in our market you can get *whatever* you want to have, and *as soon as* you want it?'

'But you have nothing to offer us,' said Self-Reliance. 'We're journeying towards what we want to *be* and *do*. But here you concentrate on selling what you believe people should *have* through peer pressure. But the reality you haven't grasped is that, though people love to buy, they hate to be sold.'

'That sounds very noble, but if the buying decision was left up to the customer no one would ever sell anything! Every shop would incur loss and our town would not exist. I see what game you're up to. You've come here to destroy us!' announced Judge Find-Fault. 'My examination of you is concluded and I have decided to send you for trial.'

'Trial?' said Chris, bewildered.

'Yes, you may think that we don't treat people here with any thought, but just to show you that you're *wrong* about us, we will allow you the benefit of a trial,' replied Judge Find-Fault. 'Even though in my opinion you're wasting our time.'

'But what are we being charged with?' asked Chris.

'Disturbance of the peace, loitering in the mall, causing unrest among the people and spying,' read Judge Find-Fault from his notes and, turning to his clerk Petty, said, 'Take them down and set the trial for tomorrow.'

'Wait,' said Chris, 'who is going to represent us?'

'The court will take care of that *service* for you,' replied Petty.

There was little light in the jailhouse, which was in the basement of the courthouse. Our pilgrims were put into separate cells that both already had an occupant.

'Ah, company at last,' said Chris's cell mate, whose name was Entrepreneur. 'What are you in here for, causing unrest or spying?'

145

'I take it you are in here under false pretences also then?' replied Chris.

'This town is unbelievable!' said Entrepreneur. 'I have never known such a place that is so full of people, yet empty of ideas. A cartel of businesses decides what they want to sell and then everyone has to buy into whatever it is, or is considered an outcast of their society. I'm from the Land of Prosperity which, to be honest, I now wish I had never left. But I was so successful there that I thought it would be a great idea to seek out other markets. This was the first place I came to, but as soon as I started suggesting rewarding customers with things they wanted, but didn't expect, I was accused of causing unrest.'

'But with our trial tomorrow, they seem keen on dealing out their odd sense of justice very quickly here,' said Chris. 'So how long have you been here? Surely they must have set a trial for you?'

'Too long, though it's been great to have the opportunity to think. And my *trial* in fact has started three times but on each occasion I have come up with an idea that they are not sure whether they like, so they have postponed sentencing me.'

'Sentence you! But how can they do that if your trial is not even finished?' exclaimed Chris in surprise.

'You will soon see that they can do anything they like. And if they think it's going to be difficult then they just create a title, or a position, so that someone can be in charge of it. The trouble is everybody is so busy giving orders, or organising meetings, that nothing really ever gets done. Apart from the fact that they seem able to put their case against you, complete with witnesses, in double-quick time. Do you know who they have defending you yet?'

'No, we don't, though from what you say it may be better to defend ourselves,' said Chris.

'Fine thought, but they won't let you,' answered Entrepreneur. 'They would accuse you of undermining their process and add it to the other charges they say you are charged with. Well, you'll either get Malevolence, though he usually prosecutes if Judge Find-Fault is unable to, as they take in turns to sit on the bench, or Stigma. Though he only attaches himself to your case at the direction of the Judge.'

'Are you saying that Judge Find-Fault prosecutes as well?' asked Chris incredulously. 'And that the prosecutor, Malevolence, is also a Judge?'

'That's right,' said Entrepreneur. 'So you can be sure of having either judgment, or grudgement, passed against you.'

'But that's utter injustice!' said Chris.

Life isn't fair in the way you would suppose it to be, all that counts is the way you live it. By choosing *how* you live will make you responsible for your actions. Personal responsibility gives you power over your future.

'Who said life was a fair game? What's up to you is how you play it,' replied Entrepreneur. 'Life isn't the way it's supposed to be, it's just the way it is. After all, three quarters of "life" is spelled lie isn't it? What makes the difference is the *way* you cope with it.'

'Well, I'm not going to live my life as a lie, whatever the demands or accusations against me. They can say what they want but I'll never recognise what they stand for,' said Chris defiantly.

'That's the spirit,' said Entrepreneur. 'Don't let them weaken your commitment, which is what they'll try to do. I have learned that commitment is not about keeping going when it's easy. Anyone can do that. It's about keeping going when it's tough, really tough and the odds are all against you. That's commitment.

'Do you know, almost every project that I have ever started has attracted ridicule,' he continued. 'It's almost as if people are determined to see my ideas fail and hope to see me fall flat on my face. Yet, I've discovered that despite all the obstacles, each time I've succeeded, those people who laughed, first began to be resentful for what I had created, and then, in due course, they started to enjoy the benefits themselves. And you know what they say when they do? They say, wasn't I lucky? Yet, when I started living in Service City, people never laughed. Moreover they wanted me to succeed and expected me to grow.'

'You actually lived there!' exclaimed Chris. 'Then what on earth possessed you to come here?'

'Well, I already told you that I was looking for new markets, in fact it was more to apply my knowledge on new markets. So that others would be able to enjoy the benefits that were enjoyed at Service City. What, of course, I didn't count on was that the people who live here are embittered because they gave up trying to get to the Land of Prosperity in the first place.'

'So, you assumed their motives to be sincere like yours, while they assumed your motives to be ulterior?' said Chris.

'That's about the picture. But I'm afraid it looks like you're in the same frame.'

On their way up to the courthouse the following morning, Chris related to Self-Reliance what he had learned from Entrepreneur.

'Well, it seems your company was somewhat more stimulating than mine,' said Self-Reliance, 'I had to share my cell with Contempt. He, too, derided the justice of this town. But he didn't stop there. He was disdainful of all justice everywhere. In fact, he poured scorn on everything, no matter what subject we discussed. He sneered at me for considering going to Service City. He jested at having such a companion as you who would get me locked up in a cell. There was nothing he didn't have a gibe against.'

'Did he say why he was there himself?' asked Chris.

'He said that the court kept putting him there because he couldn't keep his comments to himself during sessions. Mind you, his manner is so abhorrent that I believe he keeps doing it to himself.'

'Well, he's right on one thing,' sighed Chris. 'This court we're about to face is not interested in justice. How on earth are we going to get out of here?'

'It seems that we may have to keep our own counsel,' replied Self-Reliance. 'Because, whatever we say they seem intent on turning against us.'

'Quiet in the court room!' called Clerk Petty, impolitely. 'All rise for his honour Judge Find-Fault.'

'Read out the charge and let's get on,' boomed Judge Find-Fault eagerly.

'Will the accused stand,' instructed Petty. 'There are six charges, my Lord. Both offenders are charged with disturbing the peace. Loitering in the mall without any intention of buying anything. Not having sufficient funds to purchase a title, having agreed to do so. Causing unrest among the people who were engaged in going about their business. Defaming the good name of our town through slanderous accusations. And spying on behalf of persons who wish ill upon us. There is actually a seventh charge of wasting the court's time currently held in abeyance pending how the defendants plead, Your Honour.'

'And how do you plead?' enquired Judge Find-Fault frowning at the two bewildered travellers in his dock.

Having momentarily paused to get his wits together after what he had just heard, Chris said, 'Conscious of not wanting

149

to waste the court's time, would it be in order to ask to see our counsel before pleading?'

Judge Find-Fault looked at a person sitting directly opposite Clerk Petty, and raised his eyebrows. The man, who was Stigma, got out of his seat, directed his attention to the dock and addressed himself to Chris and Self-Reliance.

'I have been attached to you for the duration of this case but let me assure you that I have been fully briefed,' said Stigma, who then turning to face the Judge added, 'I am advising my clients to plead guilty as charged, Milord. On behalf of my clients I would like to ask leniency on the basis that, as it is their first time to Superficial Town and being overwhelmed by what was available here for them, they acted without thinking. On the basis that they be allowed to reside in this town, I ask on their behalf if the charges may be dropped.'

Chris could not believe what was being said and was about to shout his protest when Self-Reliance gripped his arm. 'Wait,' he whispered, 'if the only way we are going to get out of here is by escaping, then we may find it easier do so if we are not behind bars.'

'But we must be true to ourselves,' protested Chris quietly.

'But we have said nothing yet. What good will it do us to feed their prefabricated argument? It's just what they want so that more charges can be pressed against us. Their aim is to keep us here no matter how they do it. But remember what Intuition advised. He told us that we must do whatever we were able to do to get through, without compromising our values; and to keep our mind on why we wanted to get through. He didn't advise us to argue as to why they should not keep us.'

'You're right,' agreed Chris. 'Our defence, Stigma, who has been attached to us will not let anyone reasonably listen to us.'

'It is my considered opinion that we should not consider dropping the charges until we have heard from the witnesses,' said Judge Find-Fault. 'After all, we are in session at the moment, so we wouldn't want to waste the opportunity to engage in what we are good at in Superficial Town: judging people. Bring in the first witness.'

As Manipulate entered, he eyed the two he had managed to get into the dock and looked gratified. His evidence confirmed what the court wanted to hear.

'I went out of my way to please one of them,' he said, 'even to the trouble of showing him what we stood for. Yet, he was only interested in telling me what he was about, and belittled our own words. However, I persevered and offered him one of our best posts. Well, to tell the truth, he was very derogative about being a controller. He didn't even appreciate my offer to introduce him into the local community. Then he started to take me to task about not being here last week, in case there might have been something better on offer. Well, I could see that there was no pleasing him, and that people were starting to get out of his way and even leave the premises. So, in adherence of the title of Head of Customer Control, I brought him here.'

'May I ask if at any time you felt that the defendant you refer to did not have sufficient funds to purchase what he wanted?' asked Stigma.

'Not at the time but it soon became clear to me afterwards,' replied Manipulate. 'Why else would he waste my time? Furthermore, he knew he had to purchase something because I pointed out the minimum purchase above the door.'

'No further questions,' said Stigma.

The next witness was Plausible who did the same for Self-Reliance that Manipulate had done for Chris. It was clear to the defendants that his deceptive evidence was just what the court expected to hear. Plausible's testimony seemed to remind Judge Find-Fault of his examination of the two and he made a note of it while looking at Chris.

The witness following Plausible was someone whom Chris recognised from the City of Apathy.

'Yes, I've known that defendant for some years now,' said Resentment, pointing at Chris, 'and he's always been a troublemaker. He always took the best parking space at work, just because his car was better than mine. He tried to tell me that it was because he got in earlier than I did, but that wasn't the real reason. He just wanted to rub my nose in it because he had taken the position that was due to me. And that's only because I wasn't there. One week I'm away, then the next I return and he's taken it.'

'So you should have been there the previous week as he was after the best position?' asked Judge Find-Fault.

'You're telling me! Yet, all he could say was that it was nothing to do with me not being there the week before,' said Resentment. 'I left because of him, I'm sure I did. And I bet that's why he's here. He's after the position that I got here last week.'

As no questions were forthcoming from Stigma, the last witness was called. Chris also recognised him as he had encountered him on the way to Integrity House.

'He categorically refused to help me in any way whatsoever,' said Bureaucrat. 'All that my colleague and I were interested in was to ease his path, and he flatly refused to co-operate. Because of him we were left in a right mess and that wasted a whole night. It was only by sheer luck that we discovered in the morning that we must have been able to free ourselves during the night. And what was he doing out on the road so late? Spying if you ask me! Because, right after he left us, he started to snoop around a large building that was close by.'

'Just because one of my clients did not assist you, which I think we all agree that perhaps he should have done, does not make him a spy, does it?' questioned Stigma.

'That's not for me to judge is it?' answered Bureaucrat. 'All I know is what I've told you. But if you gave me the time to get him to fill out some of my forms I'm sure I could tell you much more.'

Good customer service is built on sincerity and trust, there is no place for superficiality.

'Enough!' interrupted Judge Find-Fault, 'I'll be the judge of what we decide. And though it's clear to me what this court will decide, I would like to hear from the defendants, as there are a couple of further points I want to put to them. Now,' he added looking at Chris, 'yesterday you enlightened us with how people like to buy, but not to be sold. Surely you must realise that for business to make a profit it is logical to sell things?'

'Customers buy for their own reasons not businesses' reasons,' answered Chris. 'And there are only *two* reasons that *any* customer buys anything.'

'Oh really?' enquired Judge Find-Fault sarcastically. 'And what reasons would those be perchance? Good marketing and well-packaged products no doubt. Well, we *already* know that!'

'Actually, the reasons are *good feelings* and *solutions to problems*,' said Chris.

Good feelings and solutions to problems, these are the reasons why customers buy. When customers feel good about what they're being offered and can see that it is going to be of benefit to them you will get a positive sale.

'Good feelings and solutions to problems,' said Judge Find-Fault. 'Well that's not logical at all. If business were to waste its time asking what made the customer feel good, that would mean that the customer would be dictating how even the production lines would be run. No, that would never work! People buy what's available and fortunately in our town we give them a wide choice. We know what people need. They need status, titles, as well as houses, clothes, food, insurance, computers and cars. We even know that our young customers need toys.'

'People don't want to be sold a house,' said Chris. 'They want to feel comfort and contentment, make a good investment while feeling a sense of ownership. They don't want to be sold clothes. They want to feel good about their appearance. They don't want to be sold a computer, they want to feel the benefits that technology can offer. People don't want to be sold *toys*. They want to buy *happy moments* for their children.

'All of us buy emotionally, not logically. We don't buy what we need, we buy what we want and our wants are based on feelings. All of us may need food, for example, but what we *want* is a delicious steak or some succulent fish for dinner. We use logic when we want to justify our emotional feelings. When we think about buying the car we want, we justify why it is right for us because it's reasonable to run and has lots of extras including a warranty. We buy things because they make us feel good.'

'And what about your other reason, solutions to problems?' said Judge Find-Fault. 'I suppose you're suggesting that a business must know how to define what all the problems of its customers are, so that it can provide a solution? What an impossible and ridiculous state of affairs we'd all be in if that were the case?'

'When we have a problem, none of us is looking to buy things,' answered Chris. 'We want to buy solutions to our problem. People don't need one centimetre *drill bits*, they want one centimetre *holes*. They don't want to be sold dishwashers or microwaves. They want to solve their problem of not having enough time because of inconvenient chores. People don't need mobile phones, they want instant contactability. The problem is the difference between what we have and what we want. It's up to business to serve its customers by asking them two questions. What is their current situation and how they would like it to change?

'With such questions business is able to provide solutions to problems. Every customer, of course, has a different emotional make-up and different problems need to be solved. You gain and develop loyalty with customers by giving them what they want and not what you *think* they should want.'

'You are clearly advocating that we should be spending more of our time on our customers, instead of spending it on our products, as we currently do,' said Judge Find-Fault.

'Your focus is on keeping customers coming back to your shops, isn't it?' asked Chris.

'No, our intent is to keep selling our wares to them,' replied Judge Find-Fault.

'Well, if you focus your attention on your customers they *will* come back. But if you continue to concern yourself about just your wares, you will only find that they don't come back. Success and greater profitability for your town hinges on how it rewards its customers with good feelings and solutions to problems. Forget about selling. If you concentrate on helping customers buy what's best for them they will always buy from you.'

'And you think you know what's best for our town do you, after just a short time eh? Forget about selling? You must be more deranged than we thought. Selling is what keeps us here!' boomed Judge Find-Fault.

'But you're not listening,' pleaded Chris who had genuinely believed that he had been getting through to Judge Find-Fault. 'Concentrating on how you can help your customers more is a much better principle than the practice of thinking how can I make as many sales as possible today. Don't you know that you get what you give in life? And that you have to give before you receive? And where can that be more true than in the business arena.'

'Of course I understand that. We always make sure that people give us the money before we part with our goods,' commented Judge Find-Fault.

'There's a big difference between selling and helping people to buy, you know,' returned Chris his voice rising in exasperation. 'Having the attitude of "let's take what we have and talk someone into buying it" is being nothing short of manipulative. The customer doesn't like it. On the other hand, finding out what the customer wants and matching it with what you have, ordering it, making it specifically, or sending them to where it can be obtained, is what the customer loves to hear!'

'Enough of this insolence!' shouted Judge Find-Fault. 'I denounce your arguments and find you guilty as charged on all counts. Furthermore, I am not prepared to grant any of the leniency because of the mitigation that Stigma attached to your case. You are too dangerous to live in Superficial Town because you undermine our way of life. Now what is to be done with you?'

'It has been said that you keep people who don't conform to Superficial Town life incarcerated,' said Self-Reliance. 'But to my mind my companion will still be able to influence your people. Might I suggest to your honour that we be put to death? But *please* on no account banish us from your town for that would be *too* unbearable.'

'Hmmm, I like what you suggest, but why should I not banish you both and be done with it?' replied Judge Find-Fault.

'Banishment for us would be a fate worse than death because we would be tarnished with the reputation of having been refused

Superficial life. We would have to put up with people's taunts about how stupid we were to give up the opportunity of having whatever title, status or possession we wanted immediately. I appreciate that through banishment you would be sending a clear message to the world that nothing could influence the way Superficial life operates. And though I understand that destroying us would indicate that influence, such as ours, frightens you, I would once more ask that you finish us off in Superficial.'

'Your argument is strong, but once again I refuse you leniency,' said Judge Find-Fault. 'My judgment is that you will be taken from this court immediately and forcibly *banished* from our town. And your name will be placed on posters that we will place around the town as a reminder of how *we* in Superficial remain *uninfluenced* by your ideas.'

And so it was that our two pilgrims were able to quit the deluded streets and hypocritical shops of the town that would not listen. As they were taken to the town's limits, posters were being put up proclaiming: 'Superficial is no place for Self-Reliance, or those that choose to travel with him.'

'That was brilliant of you to so confidently propose what you did,' said Chris when they were safely beyond the town's borders. 'I'm afraid I got so wound up with the whole attitude of the court that I couldn't stop myself from preaching as I did. But I really thought that they were taking on board what I was saying.'

'Your arguments were both principled and well founded but the harder you pushed them the further your listeners went away from you,' said Self-Reliance. 'I could see that the Judge was only interested in finding fault in your arguments. That's all he was looking for, so it would not have mattered what you had said.'

'That's why you requested the death penalty for us, of course. I couldn't believe my ears when I heard you suggest such a thing!'

Self-Reliance laughed. 'I knew it would dumbfound you, which was just as well because it looked as though that was what you wanted as well. Because he took the opposite approach to everything else said, in pleading my case for destroying us, which was the course he favoured, he was forced to take the alternative. It was the best choice for his town, as far as he could see.'

'But why could he not see what I was getting at?' asked Chris.

'Because, like Entrepreneur, you were trying to get him to buy into your ideas by saying things he just didn't want to hear. He believed that your ideas would make the people, his customers, more important than he was. As leader of this town, he likes the way it is and sees no reason to have it any other way. He has made all of the townspeople as judgemental as him because it is a practice that has worked so well for him and, he now considers it to be a principle worth fighting for.'

'Yes, I could see that he was unable to recognise the difference between the principle of service and the practice of selling,' said Chris.

'Few recognise that there are major differences between principles and practices,' said Self-Reliance. 'Where man-made practices, rules and conventions may differ between the City of Apathy and Service City, for instance, the principle of fire will burn in both cities with the same ferocity. A principle is uniform wherever you are, whereas a practice is variable. Any principle that we appeal to in resolving a problem, or in deciding our actions can be applied over and over again in other circumstances. A practice, however, is simply something that *may* work well for an appropriate circumstance. But often what happens is that as time goes by people believe the practice is a principle that must be followed. Whereas of course the circumstance may no longer be appropriate.'

'So where Judge Find-Fault believes he is sticking to principles, he is really only applying Superficial practices,' said Chris. 'No wonder he was not prepared even to listen to me, because I threatened what he believed to be his guiding principles?'

'Absolutely! The difference between a beehive and the human city is that wherever the bees form a hive it is the same, determined by the bees' instinct, whereas the human city develops different politics for different places, different governments and laws. And wherever rules or procedures are not in harmony with principles the consequence will be dis-harmony, as in Superficial. As principles operate regardless of our awareness of them, ignorance of them does not mean we can escape from their immutable laws.'

'The laws that Judge Find-Fault invented to suit Superficial Town have now been around for so long that I suppose he is unaware of what real guiding principles are. His selling practices have become the misguided principles that guide all of his decisions.

'Because Man does not invent principles, they apply in all situations whatever the circumstances. But because Man invents practices, whenever he experiences a difficulty he looks for his security in a practice. A prescribed way of dealing with something that previously worked in another situation. The difficulty is that when the practice does not work with a future situation this brings the feeling of incompetence. Which is why our presence threatened him, of course. When we live our lives based on principles, we can apply them in any circumstance. Understanding a practice helps us to meet the current problem sufficiently, but understanding the principle behind the practices allows us to meet future challenges actively.'

'I suppose that teaching our children practices which were suitable for our circumstances will not necessarily prepare them for the challenges they will meet in their lives,' said Chris. 'Our children, and for that matter new colleagues and customers, seem to have an inclination to ask why something is done, or has to be carried out in a particular way. Such occasions should be used as an opportunity to test a practice to see if it adheres to an underlying principle that would work in different circumstances, how effective it is as a practice and whether it can be improved. It should not be considered a time to enforce what we think is true just because it's what we have always done.'

Principles work every time, practices only sometimes. Fire is constant, man-made rules are not.

'Most principles are common sense, of course, like listening before speaking, starting at the beginning and sowing before reaping,' said Self-Reliance. 'Yet, there is a paradox to following principles. For example, when you give up trying to impress a group, you become more impressive; or a show of strength suggests insecurity, which is certainly what Judge Find-Fault and his colleagues suffer from.'

'Certainly, I have learned that your best work is done when you try to forget your own point of view and look beyond it to the wider perspective,' said Chris. 'The less you make of yourself, the more you become. I just wish I had realised this before the court case.'

'But it was your actions that brought about my insight to make me propose what I did. You were simply being true to yourself. You stuck to what you believed in and it was the values of integrity, fairness, sincerity and discipline you displayed that the Superficial people disliked. Values that are guided by those principles that are essential in developing excellence and depth of character.'

'I just wish I could have got them to see the power of the Principle of Service,' said Chris. 'That is, to always serve others in a way that you would wish to be served, for your return will always equal your service.'

'Yes, we will always be rewarded in life in exact proportion to the value of our service to others because we develop ourselves best through others,' added Self-Reliance. 'You know, I believe that being in business is a lot like playing tennis.'

'In what way?' asked Chris curiously.

'Well, those who don't learn to serve well, will always end up losing!'

To Be a Pilgrim ...

- Have the courage of your convictions
- Always follow through your ideals and goals
- View marketing as building relationships, not as a support tool for selling
- Know it is the little things that build a competent, trustworthy reputation
- Stay committed when it's really tough and the odds are all against you
- Apply Principles of Service in preference to selling practices
- Know that when you stop trying to impress you become more impressive
- Always endeavour to return more than you receive

Chapter Six

Escaping from Hesitation Castle

With Superficial Town some way behind them, Chris and Self-Reliance could once more see their way ahead. The road was narrower than before, though at least it was straight. Yet, the road's surface did not make the going easy, as it was strewn with sharp rocks that they had to pick their way through.

'Wait for us!' shouted a voice behind and turning they made out two figures coming towards them.

'They must be from Superficial Town,' said Chris, as he eyed the buildings now somewhat in the distance warily. 'Why do you think they are chasing us?'

'We'll soon learn,' said Self-Reliance, as the two figures caught them up.

The names of these two that had followed our pilgrims were Spontaneity and Impulsiveness.

'You must be twins,' said Chris as they met, 'for you appear to be so similar.'

'You're not the first to say that,' said Spontaneity. 'In fact, we bear no relation to each other at all. When I heard that Judge Find-Fault had actually allowed you your *freedom*, which is something he has never done before, the timing could not have been better for me. I was already taking voluntary action to leave Superficial.'

'Well, I only needed to see those banishment posters go up to confirm all the rumours that were so rife and spur me to action,' put in Impulsiveness. 'When I saw my neighbour here take off, I didn't waste any time reflecting, I just joined up with him.'

'But I wasn't intending to follow you,' said Spontaneity. 'But it will be an enjoyable bonus to travel with you to the Land of Prosperity, which is where I am bound.'

'Well, I'm here because of you, make no mistake,' said Impulsiveness. 'The rumours about your business principles sound like just the thing I want to be part of,' said Impulsiveness.

'I'm glad to hear that some people took notice of what I said,' said Chris.

Spontaneity looked sad as he answered, 'Not everyone wants to be in Superficial. It's just that over the past few thousand years, the vast majority of Superficial people have been acquiescent and obsequious before authority and it has become a way of life. Periodically, there have been outbursts of protest, but these have only been short-lived. Most of the time people have been sacrificing themselves so that a small minority could live in luxury.'

'It has never ceased to amaze me,' added Self-Reliance, 'that the vast majority of people continue to forfeit their individuality to be like others.'

'Fulfilling our potential,' said Spontaneity, 'and being the person we are destined to be, will only come about when we follow our true nature. To worry and fret about trivial things such as wearing the *right* clothes, living in the *right* house and driving the *right* car, is to cocoon ourselves within the culture of what others consider is best for us.'

Spontaneity looked back at the town he had just left behind him and added, 'To unquestionably copy those who follow an artificial path, that we have been persuaded to think is the only one available, is to abandon our natural path and our individuality. And, surely, if we relinquish our individuality we may as well renounce our claim to being human.'

If you forget that you are unique and take the easy way out in life by simply following others, you lose the ability to tap into your inner resources and your own individual strength.

'You do not seem to me like a native of the town now behind us,' said Chris. 'Where are you from originally?'

'Well, strange though it may sound, not one person has ever been born in Superficial, though you will have no doubt noticed there are many young children being raised there,' replied Spontaneity. 'Most of the population, including myself, just ended up there. I suppose, when we are waylaid from our true path we lose the inclination to get back on it. The worst part is that we end up spending most of our days living vicariously through others that proclaim to be on their path.

'That's what is so ridiculous about me. I was born in Frankness, not far from here, in fact. As a youth I took the Freedom Road intending to go straight to the Land of Prosperity. Well, I stopped in Superficial because I thought that I had already made it there. I didn't realise that I had been lulled into a false sense of security. I involved myself in my work – it was well paid with the promise of a good pension – and I managed to buy a property in the most prestigious area of the town, Deluded Hollow. Then, this morning I woke up and was struck by the mistakes I was making. I hadn't contented myself. I had contained myself. I wasn't doing what I wanted to do, or living where I wanted to be. I was enjoying a comfortable existence, but I wasn't fulfilling myself. I was so busy chasing my pension I had forgotten my passion. I wanted to feel passionate again about what I did and how I lived. I did not want my epitaph to read: *Died at thirty, buried at eighty*. So, I immediately decided that the next fifty years would be spent fulfilling my potential, which is why I am once more on my way to Prosperity.'

'This Prosperity place sounds just the place for me, too!' said Impulsiveness excitedly. 'I've lived in Superficial for as long as I can remember but I've always been restless there. But you'll be glad that I have joined you because I know this part of the road that we're on like the back of my hand, and you'll be pleased to learn that just ahead of us now there is a stile into Short-cut Meadow. Look, there it is now, come on!'

'I don't think we should divert from our path, even though walking on these sharp rocks is an endurance,' said Self-Reliance cautiously.

Chris, whose feet were now hurting quite considerably, looked at the path over the stile.

'You see!' shouted Impulsiveness. 'Look how that path doesn't divert from our path at all. It simply follows by the side of it.'

'They do run side by side,' said Chris to Self-Reliance. 'For so long as it does run parallel, let's take the opportunity to walk on the easier path. And if it starts to go off in a different direction we can easily get back through the hedge on to this path again.'

Self-Reliance stepped over the stile and looked at the softer path before him. With the primroses that bordered the sides it certainly looked more pleasant than the adjacent road. And it did run alongside.

'Okay, but only as far as it goes our way, said Self-Reliance.

As each of the four travellers stepped over the stile in turn they all failed to notice the broken sign that lay hidden in the hedge. Unwittingly, they had stepped directly into the State of Limbo.

They had been walking and talking for a couple of hours when Self-Reliance noticed that the hedge to the side of them had become really thick. It was so thick that it was not possible to see their former road on the other side.

'I think we'd better find a way through here or go back before we get lost,' he said to the others. 'And it will be getting dark soon.'

'Well, it seems a long way to have to go back,' said Chris feeling somewhat guilty. 'Perhaps there will be a way through any minute. Let's keep an eye out for a place where we can squeeze through.'

'Or ask someone for directions, such as that man over there,' suggested Spontaneity, pointing towards another traveller resting on the side of the bank just ahead of them.

'Excellent!' agreed Chris approaching the stranger. 'Afternoon! I see that you're going in the same direction as us. Do you know where this road leads? Does it join back up with the harder one that runs alongside?'

'It is said that this road goes to Service City,' said Rationale, for that was his name. 'As for joining up with the other road I can only say that it would be reasonable for it to do so, wouldn't you?'

'There, I told you so!' exclaimed Impulsiveness. 'Look where I have led you already.'

'Would you happen to know how much further it is?' asked Chris. 'With daylight fading it would be good to know whether we can reach it before nightfall.'

'I don't see why you shouldn't,' answered Rationale. 'But then I don't see why you should either. After all, there is bound to be an inn on this road, isn't there? It's better to stay there and arrive at Service City during the day, isn't it? I believe that there should be an inn, or guesthouse, just a little further on. Perhaps you could ask them to keep a room for me if you find one. I'm sure that they wouldn't mind doing so, would they? I'm just going to rest here a little longer because I have only just stopped. There would be no sense in going on immediately after I've just stopped, would there now?'

'Well, we could rest here with you for a few moments if you like, and then we could go on together,' proposed Chris.

'What would be the sense in that?' replied Rationale. 'You weren't going to stop and don't need a rest. You only stopped because you were unsure of where you were heading. No, it makes sense that you go ahead doesn't it?'

Feeling somewhat confused Chris joined his three companions and they continued in the growing darkness.

'I'm not sure what planet he was on,' said Self-Reliance. 'Listening to him didn't give me any confidence at all.'

'No, but it does make more sense to go on rather than go back,' said Chris. 'And anyway there's bound to be something up ahead isn't there? It stands to reason, doesn't it? Why would there not be a guesthouse on the road to Service City for weary travellers?'

'If we're not sure whether we're on the right road the only sensible thing to do is to go back, regardless of how much we have to retrace our steps,' commented Self-Reliance. 'It's perhaps because you want this to be the right road so much that you are already talking like that stranger back there.'

As none of the four travellers felt inclined to say anything to each other, they travelled in silence while it grew darker. Each of their minds was occupied with their own thoughts, not least Chris who had been stung by Self-Reliance's comments. 'It was true,' he thought, 'I do so want this to be the right road and, because of it, I am already convincing myself that there is good reason for taking it. But how do I know for certain? Intuition was precise in his guidance not to leave the straight path after leaving Superficial, despite how difficult it might become. And at the first opportunity what do I do? I take the easiest route that is offered. But that stranger did say that this would lead to Service City. Why would he say that if it were not the case? What would he gain by advising people wrongly? And he said that there must be a place to rest shortly, didn't he? Well, why would he say that if there weren't? Hmm, perhaps Self-Reliance is right. I'm even beginning to think like that stranger. How strange it is that people seem to contract doubts and fears from one another as they do illnesses.'

It is so easy to be led away from your true path when you are in a state of anxiety and have misgivings. Watch out for these states as they are so communicable.

'Look, there is a light up ahead of us, See!' Impulsiveness's shout brought Chris back instantly from his reverie.

Following the direction of the light, they soon came upon an enormous building that, in the dark, looked derelict and uninviting.

'It's just like some fortress,' said Spontaneity. 'Look at the castellated roof, and the turrets. If it's a guesthouse, it's certainly not very welcoming. In fact, I'd say it was most foreboding.'

As the four of them pondered whether to knock on the large entrance door or not, they heard a rumble of thunder and it began to spit with rain.

'It's no good vacillating, is it,' said Chris feeling as guilty of it as much as the others and wondering why he was prevaricating. 'We're going to get completely soaked if we stay here. Let's knock and ask if this is a guesthouse and if they can put us up for the night. Even if they can't help us at least they'll be able to provide us with some temporary shelter, can't they? Why shouldn't they, eh?'

Knocking on the door made an empty echoing sound within as if there were only stone walls and floors to hear it. A few moments later the door opened and there stood before them a giant of a man. He was so large that he almost completely filled the doorway and blocked out the light that was behind him.

'Good evening,' started Chris, 'we're sorry to have bothered you this evening, but we're looking for an inn or guesthouse that we were advised would be near here. We were wondering if this was it by any chance?'

The giant man looked at them solemnly with dark brooding eyes.

'It was, once,' he growled in a low voice, 'in happier times that is. Before they changed the State boundary. Suppose it still is, in a way. Though travellers are few and far between, more's the pity.'

With a loud crack of lightning followed by an almost instantaneous clap of thunder, the heavens opened and the rain poured down.

'Would it be possible to shelter anyway, at least until the rain stopped?' requested Chris.

For a moment the giant before them looked as if he was preoccupied with thoughts of long ago. His eyes seem to bore right through the four huddled around his doorway, as if they weren't there. The next moment, he stepped back and pulled the door wide open. Each of the four travellers felt as if reproachful eyes were following them as they entered into what was a large hallway. The giant pushed the heavy entrance door shut, turned the lock and pocketed the key.

'Follow me,' he growled and led the way down the corridor to a large reception hall. Chris could see that in former times this had been a sumptuous and elegant room. But the heavy drapes that hung around it were now jaded, worn and dusty. There was dust everywhere. The backs of the large wing chairs that faced the fireplace, the tables, the picture and the bookcases were all in need of a clean. One of the tables looked as though it had been hewn out of stone. On its surface rested a large book that had clearly not been opened for a very lengthy period.

'No one's touched this place for years,' Chris said quietly to Self-Reliance.

'Let's have your passes then,' boomed their enormous host. 'I shouldn't have let you in without them, but it was your fault for reminding me of the old days.'

Chris looked at the bewildered faces staring at him.

'We're not certain what you mean by passes,' said Chris.

'Your passes! Everybody must have a pass. It's the law! It's not my fault that they changed the boundary. But it's more than my job's worth not to see your passes. Come on!' he growled.

'I've lost mine tonight,' lied Impulsiveness. 'But I'm sure I'll find it tomorrow when it's light.'

'That's no excuse! It's hardly my fault that you've gone and been careless, is it? There's no way I'm going to have condemnation against me just because of your neglect in looking after your pass. Everyone knows that here in the State of Limbo it's against the law to do anything without a pass.'

The giant's eyes glared at them. 'So that's why you tricked me into letting you in, just so that you could get me into trouble! Well it's unfair and totally reprehensible to put me in a position where I can be accused of not doing what I'm meant to be doing. Stay here and don't move!'

The four men stood there stunned at what had just been said to them as the large man stormed out of the room.

'I can't believe what's happening here,' said Chris. 'And what on earth are we doing in the State of Limbo, of all places? Is this a guesthouse or not? And who is this person who seems intent on calling others to count for everything?'

'Hesitation Castle is where you are and Giant Blame is your host,' said a voice from behind one of the large winged chairs.

'And, yes, you are in the sorry State of Limbo, which you must have entered illegally, otherwise you would have a pass,' said a second voice from behind another chair.

The two people who had spoken got out of their chairs and came forward to introduce themselves. The one who had spoken first was Attentive. She explained how she had heeded a request from the State to help with improving communication lines to neighbouring provinces. She had been sent a pass and had stopped off at Hesitation Castle because it was the nearest place to the border shared with the Ground of Good Fortune.

The other was named Indignant, who did actually reside in the Limbo and did have a pass, but unfortunately *had* lost it that day. He was livid that Giant Blame had taken him to task so much for what was surely a common error and even more angry because the 'oaf', as he had put it, would not let him go until he showed him his pass.

'And how can I show him something I haven't got?' said Indignant. 'It really is too bad! And what's worse is that I have to pay for my room as long as I stay here, even though the oaf insists on keeping me here! He keeps on about it not being his fault and that they should never have changed the State boundary. Absolute poppycock, that's what I say!'

'But what does he mean by that?' asked Chris. 'It's almost the first thing he said to us. He appears to be very annoyed about whatever it is.'

'Well, a long time ago Hesitation Castle was actually the entrance to the Ground of Good Fortune—' began Attentive.

'We're that close!' interrupted Chris.

'Well, you were that close but, since the change, this castle now lies on a different path,' replied Attentive.

Chris stole a sorrowful look to Self-Reliance who was standing next to him and said quietly, 'I'm so sorry for leading you off the path when we were so close. I should have known better. Please forgive me.'

Self-Reliance smiled and said, 'Forget it, I already have. I know that your motives were good.' Turning to Attentive he asked her, 'Why was the State boundary changed?'

'Now, there's a story in itself,' she began. 'Legend holds that this castle used to be a fine place where enthusiastic travellers on their way to Prosperity would enjoy a very brief sojourn before finally entering the Ground of Good Fortune. For pilgrims who had been committed to leaving their existing world of Mediocrity it was like an oasis of thankful refreshment. It offered a precursor of the lifestyle they would experience if they stayed firm to their resolve and true to their commitment. And, of course, if they acknowledged that success could only come about through service to others and helping others to become successful. It was more a passing out academy, than anything else I suppose. Its motto was: *He who hesitates is lost*, adhering to the philosophy that the individual who knows what they stand for, has firm values for guidance, follows their heart and is able to align what they do with what they are, will *never* hesitate.

Knowing your own mind and being comfortable with who you are means that seizing the moment will be natural for you.

'Now you may have noticed that this academy was built like

a fortress. And the reason for that was very simple. Those who were on their way to reaching Prosperity understood that there were two further elements that were required to harness all the key attributes of an individual for continuous and successful growth. These were leadership and teamwork. And only those who were able to work together towards a shared purpose were able to find their way out of the fortress, enter Good Fortune and go forward to Prosperity. Pilgrims who were unable to work with like-minded others and did not act with the attributes of a leader, when under pressure, would simply show their falseness through their doubts about what to do. Their hesitation therefore would be their downfall.

'Things started to go wrong, however, when certain travellers used their energy to get around their true path, instead of simply following it. Many reached here that were unsure of their motives, did not know what they stood for, had not established their values and had no idea about aligning their personal mission with their professional one. But they still wanted the benefits that Good Fortune offered. The numbers of these fair-weather pilgrims grew into an unwelcome force that would not leave. Wanting the benefits of success without paying the price in advance, they misused the advantages that were available here and created anarchy. Many diligent pilgrims lost their hope and then their way because people despised them for having the courage of their convictions. In the anarchy that followed, the fair-weather pilgrims littered the straight and narrow road with sharp stones on the basis that if they could not get Good Fortune, then no one else should be able to either. So Prosperity altered the boundary.

'It was a simple thing to do,' continued Attentive, 'because they saw the real success in reaching their land was more of a journey than actually a destination. So they gave a huge part of the land of Good Fortune to the State of Limbo for those people who wanted to periodically enjoy a part of it, but were unable to get to Prosperity. They left the road littered with its obstacles taking the simple view that such a road would still build leadership and teamwork attributes for dedicated pilgrims. Notwithstanding, of course, that there was no longer the symbol that this fortress had formerly provided.

'Well, you can imagine how absolutely delighted the misguided pilgrims were with themselves. But, as they had done nothing to deserve it, what they had achieved did not hold value for them. Even though they at first convinced themselves that they had finally got just what they really wanted, they still allowed this great building to fall into disrepair.

'As for Giant Blame, he was one of the original pilgrims who blamed Prosperity for making entry too difficult for certain people. He, and his companions, were convinced that they were being penalised and were determined to never let go of the lifestyle that they had got used to here. Mind you, they say that he wasn't always a giant of a man. Apparently, after countless years of nourishing himself on the negative feelings that the world was out to get him, and never letting go of the resentment that built up within him, he just grew and grew. Unfortunately though, he remained small-minded, never accepting that it is up to the individual to make a contribution in life and not the other way around.

Life is not accountable to us, we are accountable to life.

'I don't know whether what they say is true or not, but the fact is that he seems unable to leave here now. He continually thinks about how things could have been for him and doesn't say much, apart from how unfair it is that such things did not transpire. Of course, with his job of checking the passes that the State of Limbo insists you carry, he has found a purpose in line with the temperament he has grown. And why the "passes" you may want to know? They are simply to indicate to the State that you *know* your place. Anyone not carrying such a pass will be considered a threat, because without one they must be holding aspirations above their station, and must be considering leaving Limbo.'

'Well, I have no such aspiration!' Indignant said. 'I'm very happy with my place here and it's an absolute outrage that such an oaf is preventing me from staying here of my own free will!'

'Don't you mean *leaving* here of your own free will,' offered Spontaneity.

'I'm quite aware of what I mean, thank you very much, and the last thing I need is another busybody telling me what I mean or don't mean.' With that Indignant left the room, while mumbling something about making someone pay under his breath.

Chris felt somewhat downhearted. To hear that he had been so close to Good Fortune and had once more taken himself off the right path hit him hard. Worse than that, he had ignored Self-Reliance's caution and led his companion into this lion's den. Still, the fact was that he was here and he must now concentrate on what he must do next and not dwell on past mistakes. What was it he had learned, that blame looks backward, only solutions look forward?

'Well, some of us do have aspirations to get out,' Chris said to Attentive while glancing at Self-Reliance. 'Are you able to offer any suggestion on how we can?'

Never look backwards with blame when you can look forward to solutions.

'Getting out is not going to be easy. I'm sure you noticed

that Giant Blame pocketed the key for the door through which you entered,' answered Attentive. 'Furthermore, this place really is like a fortress – even all the windows have bars, and the ones that do not are too narrow for anyone to pass.'

'There must be some other entrances,' Self-Reliance put in. 'What about the ways that those pilgrims working in teams left by?'

'I understand that false pilgrims discovered a few of them by trying to follow committed crusaders. Then for some misguided reason they blocked them up. But they can't have found them all.'

'Then it's obviously worth trying to find them, and we will,' said Chris defiantly.

'It's probably your best course of action, for you definitely must get out. There is no way that Giant Blame will let you go without a pass. He is able to provide you with one himself, but not until at least one year has passed,' said Attentive flatly.

'One year!' cried Impulsiveness. 'What does he expect us to do in the meantime?'

'Quite simply he expects you to be his paying guests which, even if you have to stay here a couple of days, is no holiday, I assure you. The lady of the house is called Taunt and even though she is supposedly your hostess, there is no pleasing her. But you will soon learn this since the serving of dinner is imminent.'

'At least we're being fed,' said Chris looking on the positive side. 'But tell me, do you know how we are to go about finding one of the old routes?'

'No, I'm afraid I can't help you there. Even if I did know their exact location it would be no good because you have to find them yourselves. The only thing that may help though is that in the old days, as you know, pilgrims were advised to lead their way to freedom and fortune as a team.' At that moment a loud dinner gong sounded. 'Ah,' added Attentive, 'dinner is about to be served. Come on.'

'But Giant Blame told us to stay here,' said Impulsiveness.

'That's only so he can reproach you later for not having done so. But as he will still charge you for dinner even if you don't eat it, you'd better come along. It's a no win house he runs here, you know. Improving communication lines? I've certainly got my work cut out in the State they're in, haven't I?'

'You would have thought that they would at least clean the place,' commented Chris as he walked along the corridor that led from the reception hall to what was supposedly the dining room. 'With a bit of effort this place would look fantastic.'

'Yes, you can just imagine how this place used to be when the people that ran it did so because they wanted to,' answered Self-Reliance. 'People perform the best and deliver the best service when they like what they do. It is clear that our hosts detest what they do, but are determined to hang on to what they have like a terrier with a bone. That's probably why the place looks as if it has been buried a few times!'

Dinner was an experience that Chris would never forget. At the time, he found it hard to remember that he was actually a paying guest. The only analogy he could possibly imagine was that he was in prison. In a way he thought he was a captive, paying for the crime of not having what it takes. Or even having what it takes, he wasn't certain. In fact, the atmosphere in Hesitation Castle filled him with uncertainty and lack of confidence. 'Little wonder you're granted a pass after one year in this place. You would be such a former husk of yourself that it's all you'd ever want,' he said to himself.

Chris could see that Indignant had been seated in the corner and was sharing a table with another diner called Irritable. It was plain to see that Indignant was not happy about having to share and, between exchanging heated words with his fellow diner, was vigorously trying to attract the attention of one of the two people serving. One of these was called Lazy and the other Slow. Neither of them appeared to know what they were doing.

'It's no good skulking over there you know!' bellowed a voice and, turning in the direction of it, Chris saw a large woman with a scornful face beckoning them towards her.

'That must be the lady of the house,' said Impulsiveness. 'Come on we'd better do what she says.'

Chris could see that Attentive had already gone straight to a table and so started to follow her.

'You'll sit where you're told to, young man,' bellowed Taunt. 'How many of you are there anyway?'

'There are four of us but we would like to sit with that lady over there,' Chris answered pointing towards Attentive. 'Have you a table for five please.'

'Five! Five! Who do you think you are? My goodness me. All I can say is that it's just as well we can't always have what we want isn't it?' scoffed Taunt. 'Whoever heard of five sitting together. Can't you see that all the tables are laid out to fours, twos and ones? There isn't a table for five!'

'There is a table of six over there, which would be fine,' offered Chris.

'But there aren't *six* of you are there? No. I'll tell you where you can sit. I can see *you* must be the visitors without passes. Well, if you think you're going to cause trouble *here* you'd better think again. This is *my* domain and you ought to count yourself lucky for eating here.'

The four companions were seated at a table and after five minutes were asked by Slow what they wanted. Upon hearing that they had not yet chosen because they did not know what was available, Slow went over to Lazy who a few minutes later returned with a menu.

179

When Slow came back after what seemed an eternity the four learned that the choices were not available, but they could have the roast. Slow and Lazy delivered the meals, at different times, and unfortunately did not return with clean cutlery until the meal was cold. This was not difficult because the food had been served on cold plates. Such a travesty of dining continued throughout the meal until Giant Blame showed them to their rooms, where they were at last allowed to freshen up, after they had paid for their dinner and board.

'It's not my fault that you came as late as you did, is it?' he had boomed when they had asked about their rooms. As for them complaining about their meal, all they heard was his incessant muttering about people without passes these days and bemoaning why such a thing had to happen to him, of all people.

Each of their guestrooms had names instead of numbers. Chris and Self-Reliance were given the room named Leadership and Spontaneity and Impulsiveness were shown into a room called Team-Building. Because it was the biggest the four agreed to meet in the Team-Building Room, in order to discuss their escape. First they took the opportunity to freshen up.

As Chris was waiting for Self-Reliance, he looked at the numerous pictures that hung around the walls. The first one was of a man entering into a large building and leading three others behind him. The words inscribed were:

> *Leadership is a commonplace activity that can be developed in ourselves, yet in looking for that which we expect to see we do not always realise this. It is a transaction entered into and maintained voluntarily based on mutual trust, respect and communication.*

The second picture showed two men, but they were one

and the same. One appeared to be following the other while the second was gazing directly out of the picture with eyes that seemed to look at Chris regardless of where he stood, to the front or either side of the picture.

The inscription read:

> Do not expect to lead others before you can
> direct yourself, for the best leaders are followers
> of truth. People become their own leaders
> when they are in command of themselves.
> You will become your own leader when you
> become true to yourself.

The third picture was of a man pulling a chain through water, with the words:

> Like water, true leaders are yielding, knowing that their followers
> do so without resistance or pressure. Leaders do not push, they
> pull through example, knowing that you don't push chain links for
> direction, you pull them for alignment. In this way leaders recognise
> the weak link that impedes the strength of the whole chain.

Chris crossed the room to look at the fourth picture. It was of a man holding a set of balance scales while looking through a window. The inscription read:

> Knowing that it is not possible to look through a window that has
> only been cleaned on one side, the true leader will neither attack
> nor defend, but will weigh both sides of any situation. Such a leader
> pays equal attention to all disputes and is aware of prejudices in
> judgement.

A fifth picture was of a man walking through a wall to a

magical land beyond. In one hand he carried a scroll, in the
other a bag of gold.

On this picture the inscription read:

*There is nothing that can withstand the true leader whose deeds
match his words. Such a person does not lead for the sake of
money or praise yet receives both in abundance. The true leader
communicates the vision of the way forward that leads to fortune
and freedom.*

'You know these pictures are really unusual,' said Chris to
Self-Reliance. 'They give sound advice, but they do *more* than
that. There is something about them that is compelling. Here,
come and take a look.'

Self-Reliance began to read each inscription as Chris had
done. 'Well, they certainly hold words of wisdom, but then this
room *is* called Leadership so they probably just follow the room's
theme. It's the same man in every picture, though the context of
the picture is unusual.'

Chris looked again at the last picture of the set. 'But look at
the last words over here: "... *the way forward that leads to fortune and
freedom.*" Isn't that exactly what we want? Once we escape from
Hesitation Castle we can enter the Ground of Good Fortune! I
believe that the pictures are revealing a way out of here. Perhaps
one of the old ways that the resourceful pilgrims were meant to
discover.'

'Well, I can't make head nor tail of them now,' replied
Self-Reliance. 'Come on, let's go and meet with the others.
They may have similar pictures.'

In the Team-Building Room, Spontaneity had also been looking
at the room's pictures, but he was unable to extract any meaning

from them. But he felt certain they, too, were hiding some message. The first picture showed the world, split into four parts. Each part occupied a corner of the picture. In the centre was a man holding a scroll in one hand and a broken chain link in the other.

The poetic inscription read:

> When his world is fragmented, what is the value of man's law?
> In wholeness the parts are greater,
> for together everyone achieves more.
> Agreement of agenda is in the hands of all,
> though the weakness of one will make harmony fall.

The second picture depicted two scenes. The first was of the same man struggling to push a stone. On top of the stone lay a closed book. To the side of him stood three other men who appeared to be indifferent to his struggles. The second scene showed the book, now open, and the four people holding the stone above their heads with ease.

The inscription read:

> When communication is shut, what strength has a man?
> Such weakness will never fulfil a plan.
> When open and clear, a man is stronger than a fort,
> for nothing can resist him when there is willing support.

The third and final picture depicted the same four people as the previous scene. All of them were sitting in a circle. But they neither sat on seats, for there were none, nor on the floor. Each person was supported on the knees of the person behind him. Upon each of their heads they wore a crown of laurel leaves. In the centre of their circle was a gold cup with four handles that each member of the circle held.

The picture's inscription read:

> *With shared objectives respite is always*
> *near and heavy work becomes light.*
> *Against such unified purpose there can be little fight.*
> *When mutual recognition and respect to each is served,*
> *the rewards for endeavour are justly deserved.*

Having tried to interest Impulsiveness in the pictures, but to no avail, Spontaneity was pleased to see that upon entering their room Chris immediately went to read the inscriptions.

'This is hardly the time to become art critics,' Impulsiveness said restlessly. 'How are we going to get back home, that's what I want to know?'

'Look,' said Chris to Self-Reliance, beckoning him towards the pictures. 'These three have the same cryptic scenes as the one in our room. I feel certain that they contain some answer to how we can escape.'

'The same man appears in these pictures as in our room, but again they're probably just here because they go with the room's theme,' Self-Reliance replied.

'But think about what Attentive told us,' said Chris. 'That in the old days pilgrims could lead their way out as a team to *freedom* and *fortune*. Well, we're going to the Ground of Good *Fortune* when we escape from here, aren't we!' Chris bit his lip as he made a mental note to stop repeatedly sounding like the stranger that had directed them. 'Everything I say I am rationalising,' he thought. 'I must be more certain when I speak, for my words make me sound doubtful.'

'And the words in one of the pictures in our room said the same thing,' put in Self-Reliance.

'Then let's study all the pictures in both the rooms, and work over them together. That way, if there is some meaning to them, we can decipher it!' said Spontaneity.

'Well, don't count me in,' Impulsiveness said impetuously. 'I'm exhausted so there's no way I'm not going to sleep. I'd be at home now if you hadn't influenced me.'

'But look here,' said Chris as he began to reread the first picture. 'These words tell us that *"together everyone achieves more"*. If you take the first letters of each word, you spell TEAM! Come on, this is no time to be tired. We must work together.'

'Well I don't want to!' shouted Impulsiveness, while turning over on the bed he had been lying on. 'You got us into this mess with all your conflicting ideas in Superficial Town. So, as far as I'm concerned, it's up to you to get us out of here.'

Chris flushed, as he wanted to argue that it had been nothing to do with him that Impulsiveness had followed him. Moreover, it was the man's own recommendation that they had taken the road that they did. But he stopped himself from reacting. This is not the way a true leader would act, he thought: a leader wouldn't react. If that first picture were true, he realised, and leadership was within him, then he must act as though it were. And how can I expect him to want to follow me if I do not sound certain of myself? That second picture said that a leader must be in command of himself. If I am to lead everyone *out* of here, where they have followed me, then I must build their belief in me, not their doubt in me. But what was it that other picture said: '*Recognise the weak link that impedes the strength of the whole.*' I must be careful that I do not allow this person's doubts to permeate us all. Or, is it my own uncertainty? Why should I think that I could lead the others? Self-Reliance is most assuredly his own man and Spontaneity has a creative strength that any leader would be proud to have. Let it be their choice to decide who is leader. For now I must lead myself by following my heart. And my heart tells me I must discourage any unrest.

Going over to Impulsiveness, he said, 'Whatever your

reasons were for leaving Superficial Town, it means a great deal that you took the action you did in following me. For I know that you put yourself at risk of being mocked by Superficial people. And I appreciate that when our feet were aching you were enthusiastic in your suggestion for us to take an easier route. For my part, I accept full responsibility for us actually taking it and indeed for leading everyone here into the predicament we are now in. Yet, even though we are all tired, I sincerely believe that it is unwise for us to do nothing and just wait for some uncertain fate.

'We must take action ourselves and we must do so now. In this way, we will dispel our doubts and be the master of our own destiny. When we get out of here I promise that we will go straight back to the turnstile where we turned off our former path. At that point you will be able to choose which way you want to go. Should you choose to return, you must blame me for leading you out of the town. Should you decide to continue with us, you will be more than welcome. But right now I need your help. We all need your help. And though I don't yet know the full significance of these pictures, look at what the third in your room says. It advises that *"with shared objectives respite is always near and heavy work becomes light"*. Well, we all share a common objective. To leave this place before the service kills us! Come on, with your valued input we will be able to decipher the full significance that is hidden from us and be free.'

At this, Impulsiveness simply nodded, got up and went straight towards the first picture. 'Come on all of you,' he said, 'let's get on with it.'

The atmosphere that had a few moments before weighed heavy in the room was now instantly transformed into an infinitely more light-hearted one. Both Self-Reliance and Spontaneity regarded Chris with genuine respect and admiration.

'We're with you,' they said in unity as they both went towards the pictures.

* * *

During the night, the four studied the notes that they had independently made from observing the eight pictures from the Leadership and Team-Building rooms.

'It strikes me that the pictures reveal first and foremost the importance of leadership attributes in developing a strong team. But there must be a second meaning to the pictures.'

'It's as though the chain, window, scales, scroll and gold are symbols for something,' added Impulsive.

'Well, the man that leads everyone into the building in picture one is the same man that walks through a wall in picture five. I believe that the building is this castle and that the wall which appears solid is actually a way out, though that probably doesn't make much sense,' said Spontaneity.

'The second Team-Building picture refers to a fort,' said Chris. 'Do you remember how Attentive referred to this place as being built like a fortress? Well, somehow by putting together all our strength we become stronger than the fort, because it cannot contain us. Perhaps the stone that can't be pushed by the one man is to be lifted by us all. That could be the wall we pass through.'

'But how could we all pass through with a stone above our heads unless something holds it there, assuming there is a wall or stone that must be moved?' asked Impulsiveness.

'Perhaps a chain is pulled to lift it!' said Spontaneity. 'One picture shows pushing does not work and another says "*don't push chain links for direction, pull them for alignment*".'

'It will be dawn soon,' said Chris. 'I propose that we explore as much as we can to see if anything we come across bears any resemblance to the symbols in the pictures.'

'But the light is not that good to see yet and not only that, but this castle is enormous. We could easily get lost,' said Impulsiveness.

'It would be better if we could find a plan,' suggested Self-Reliance. 'Perhaps Attentive would know if one exists.'

'A plan! Of course,' said Chris. *When communication is shut, such weakness will never fulfil a plan*, are among the words inscribed. There must be a plan of this fortress in a book and I know where! Come on we won't get lost just going back to Reception Hall where we met the other guests staying here.'

Making their way quietly past the dining room, through the corridor and back to the Reception Hall was easier than they imagined as a few lights had been left on. Upon entering the hall, Chris headed straight for the large stone table he had noticed upon his arrival. The book that lay on it was covered in dust.

'See a closed book upon a stone,' whispered Chris. 'You can't get much closer to the picture than that.' Opening it carefully Chris could see that it was like a large encyclopædia.

'Look for a map or plan of the place,' suggested Impulsiveness. 'There must be something that will help us.'

Chris looked under 'P' for plan, 'M' for map, and 'C' for communication to no avail.

'It doesn't look as though what we expected to see is here,' said Impulsiveness.

'What did you say? asked Chris. 'Those words ring a bell. Someone read out from our notes.'

'This is it,' said Self-Reliance. *'Leadership is a commonplace activity in ourselves, but in looking for that which we expect to see we do not always realise this.* Look under "L".'

Chris quickly turned to 'L' but again nothing was forthcoming. 'Wait a minute, it's telling us to look for leadership in ourselves. That means "O".' Chris turned to 'O' and immediately saw a huge circle filling the page. At the top of the circle there was a flame. Just in front of the flame there were steps. To the right side of the circle was a stone.

'This must be it!' said Chris excitedly.

'But it doesn't even look like a map, let alone the plan of the fortress we're in,' said Impulsiveness as he waved his hands around the room. 'Hang on, look at this room we're in. It's almost a perfect circle, isn't it?'

'And that flame must be indicating the position of the fireplace which is at the top of the room,' put in Self-Reliance.

'In which case there must be a hidden doorway, but there's no stone where it should be,' said Spontaneity.

'This must be the stone! It's just in the wrong place,' said Chris and he started to push it.'

'*Such weakness will never fulfil a plan,*' said Spontaneity. 'We have to do it together.' Though the four tried to push, the stone table was too heavy to budge.

'It's not working,' said Chris breathlessly. 'We must not be doing it right. There must be a way of lifting it. After all, didn't one of the pictures show the stone above their heads? One of us stand guard, we'll put the lights on so that we can see better.'

With the lights on a series of pictures became visible above the fireplace. 'Look at those pictures,' said Self-Reliance, 'they must be of Caesar of Rome standing in the four parts of his empire. He's wearing a laurel crown in every one.'

'And look at the one that must depict Rome itself,' said Chris. 'He is holding a scroll in one hand. That must be telling us something.'

'Yes, because *his world was fragmented* and his closest people turned on him in the end *so what was the value of his law,*' said Spontaneity.

'But he isn't holding anything in his other hand,' added Impulsiveness, who had left the corridor he was guarding to look at the picture.

'No, but he *is* pointing and that could be the *link in the chain* we must follow,' said Chris. 'What is he pointing at?'

The four of them followed the direction of Caesar's pointing arm and hand. On the opposite side of the wall, set into a deep former window-ledge, was a large earthenware pot.

'A window that you can't see through,' said Chris.

Rushing over they discovered it to be full of water. But they could see something glinting inside. Chris reached into the water and pulled out a chain. Pulling it carefully out, four further chains were revealed each with a gold handle.

'Golden handles like on the gold cup in the picture!' said Spontaneous.

'Come on, we must pull them together,' said Chris.

As they began to pull together there was a loud grating noise. The whole slab of floor, upon which the stone table stood, slowly began to rise.

'Wait!' said Impulsiveness, 'we must stop. Giant Blame must have heard such a loud noise and will be down here any moment to investigate.'

'He who hesitates is lost!' shouted Chris. 'We cannot afford to wait, now pull!'

With the four pulling the stone floor and table continued to slide easily across the room. As it did so the part of the floor directly in front of the fire also slid back revealing steps. Chris looked at Impulsiveness who was no longer pulling on his handle. *Recognise the weak link that impedes the strength of the whole,* were the words that came to him. Just in time he grasped at Impulsiveness's chain with his other hand as it was let go by Impulsiveness.

'The stones must be counterbalanced, like the scales were in the picture!' shouted Chris. 'Quick we'll only have a few moments before our escape exit closes. Go!'

Spontaneity and Self-Reliance ran for the steps in front of the fire while Impulsiveness froze. 'But how do we know for certain that it is an exit! We might be imprisoned down there for ever!' he protested.

At that moment, the booming voice of Giant Blame was heard to call out from down the corridor.

'Come on! Follow me!' shouted Chris who ran straight for the steps, pulling Impulsiveness with him. Almost as soon as they reached the bottom of the steps the stone entrance swung back to its former position. The light was not good but the air on their faces told them that the outside could not be far away.

With their adrenalin keeping them going, not a word was said as they made their way together through their dark passage. The faint noise that they had all been aware of, but kept silent about, became louder and louder. In a short while their path was blocked by a wall of water that sparkled before them because of the morning sunlight that was clearly shining beyond it.

'So this is what it means to walk through a wall to freedom,' said Chris to the others as he went to go through the waterfall first. 'And now to fortune. Come on!'

To Be a Pilgrim ...

- Remain unconcerned about trivial things, what others think you *should* do
- Do not live vicariously through others
- Chase your passion, not your pension
- Apply your energy to the task ahead, not to get around what has to be done
- Recognise the weak link that impedes the strength of the whole
- Do not be deceived by what you perceive
- Ensure you have both a personal and a customer service ethos
- Focus on opportunities, not on obstacles

Chapter Seven

Entering the Ground of Good Fortune

'This is not the first time that I have had to retrace my steps,' said Chris to Self-Reliance, as the four of them made their way back to the turnstile. 'And on each occasion it could have been avoided simply by focusing more on where I am going.'

'Awareness is everything,' replied Self-Reliance. 'But do not be too hard on yourself for our unwanted detour provided the opportunity to develop both attention and intention.'

'And to develop our leadership attributes and team-building skills, which I had not realised were so critical to success,' said Chris. 'Learning how to direct yourself through leadership builds character and the individual's strength of character is the best input he, or she, can bring to a team.'

'I found having an agreement about what we wanted to achieve was important to me,' said Spontaneity. 'For, when the time came to act, and act quickly, we did so knowing that we were all together.'

'I wish I had seen the importance of such a thing,' put in Impulsiveness, 'but, when it became important that we stick together as a team, I lost faith and thought that we were done for. I'm afraid I had to be dragged along.'

'But the input you gave in deciphering the inscriptions was important,' said Chris.

'Maybe, but I feel certain that you three would have worked them out without me, and you will reach Prosperity,' said Impulsiveness.

'Are you not coming with us then?' asked Chris.

'Much as I would like to continue journeying with you, I don't think that I'm ready for such a place yet,' replied Impulsiveness. 'You three are all confident about what you want and why you want it. But, I don't know what is important to me and indeed, to be honest, I only came along because I was externally influenced and got excited about doing something different. But what is the point of doing something different if you don't know why you're doing it? I realise now that it is important to be internally motivated, so I'm going to take some time to discover what it is that will really motivate me.'

'Will you go back to Superficial?' asked Spontaneity, as the turnstile that led back to their former path came into view.

'I don't think taking a step back will do me any good. No, I think I'll visit some friends who live in the State of Chaos. They say that many people who have lived there for a short while leave there with a firm sense of direction. Perhaps that's just the environment I need. Who knows, we may meet each other again one day, eh?'

'It has been said that out of chaos comes a dancing star,' said Chris. 'One that is full of energy and brings new life to all it influences. I believe that we all have star qualities, the secret is for us each to discover, use, channel and share them. I also believe that we will meet again.'

'Look,' interrupted Spontaneity whose eye had caught sight of something on the side of the path as they had reached the turnstile. 'It's the signpost for the State of Limbo.'

'Well, no wonder we overlooked it, thrown in the hedge like that,' said Self-Reliance. 'And I'd say that it was hidden on purpose. Perhaps in the hope that it would distract people from their path.'

'Perhaps,' answered Chris, 'but in all honesty, it was our own fault. Come on, let's put it back anyway. At least it will warn others that what may look like the primrose path is actually more dangerous than the true road to Prosperity, which is strewn with obstacles.'

> Learning leadership attributes builds
> character, which is the best input you can
> bring to a team.

Having said their goodbyes to Impulsiveness, the remaining team of three now continued along their original path. Despite the frequent obstacles before them, none of them complained. Firm in their shared sense of direction they took the opportunity to reflect on their recent experiences and to appreciate what they had learned.

'What doesn't break you certainly makes you! Obstacles don't obstruct, they instruct. So long as we become aware of how, why and where they have come about,' said Chris. 'How I could ever have imagined that I would be able to learn Enlightened Service without embarking on a process of personal development, I just don't know. The two go together like a hand and a glove. What is the use of a customer service ethos, without an awareness of a personal ethos?'

'Exactly, but then ask most companies what their customer service ethos is and they will look at you blankly. Unless they copy it from a competitor, most businesses just don't have one,' said Self-Reliance.

'And how can a marketing strategy be effective if the creators of it are not in tune with themselves or their customers? Unless we are prepared to invest our genuine emotional energy in what we do, how will we ever develop the right behaviour and attitudes for the people we serve? We can't unless we become, and want to become, attentive to their needs. Learning to pay complete attention to customers has to be the key for developing customer loyalty,' added Chris.

'The biggest challenge for everyone involved in service has got to be to keep their mind on the person they are either serving, or are there to serve,' said Spontaneity. 'People are just not trained to do so. I know that Superficial Life is not a good example to use perhaps, but just before I left there I visited my bank. Although I got there early I was not the first in the queue. When the doors opened I followed the customers ahead of me to the counter that was open. Though there were several other counters none of them were manned. Behind the screen other members of staff were either chatting or shuffling papers. I tried to get their attention but none of them looked beyond the screen. Eventually, I rang the bell at the Enquiry counter whereupon one member of staff, who actually did seem busy, came over because her colleagues, who were busy talking, ignored it. But then she tried to redirect me back to the queue, instructing me to wait. It's only because I became difficult that she then begrudgingly dealt with me. But I experienced no attentive feeling towards me. I was just another transaction that had to be processed. One who had taken her away from what she had to do under false pretences. "This is for enquiries, not processing," she had said.'

'It's amazing how many people in the service industry think that customers are just there to be a nuisance. Annoyances that behave as if they own the place and are out to cause trouble. It's as though people either forget, or don't realise, who pays their salaries,' said Chris. 'Sometimes they are entirely unaware of the customer before them. No one likes to be ignored but when you ignore a customer you might as well just dehumanise them.'

'But on those rare occasions when you meet someone who

genuinely pays you attention, don't you feel on top of the world? Isn't it terrific! You spend the whole day feeling good, because another person has emotionally energised you with their sincere and full attention,' said Self-Reliance.

'Listen! This will be the basis of our customer ethos!' exclaimed Chris and as he spoke he wrote down the words: *'Taking a genuine interest in our customer, so that we can sincerely deliver the very best attention; emotionally energising them with good feelings because we make it clear that we like them, and enjoying the opportunity to offer great service to them.*

'Just think what an incredible business we would have, irrespective of what we provided, with such an ethos that injected such positive energy into every single transaction.' Chris continued, 'Remember people don't want to be sold to, but they like buying. And they buy people not things. That's what develops customer loyalty. *Genuinely making them feel good for buying from you and by serving them with the solutions that they want.'*

'Such a business could only grow in strength, both in customers and reputation,' replied Self-Reliance. 'Such a business would be welcomed in Service City if we were to live there.'

'Then, when we get there, let's do just that!' proposed Spontaneity.

Absorbed in the firming up of a vision of what they wanted to do, encapsulating their purpose into a meaningful mission with values and guiding principles, and developing their strategy in line with a customer focused ethos, they did not notice that the road had become progressively easier. The rough ground beneath their feet had become smooth and the surrounding country was much more verdant and rich. The more they planned, the more unified, communicative and enthusiastically confident they became as individuals and as a team. Unconcerned about what obstacles may lie ahead of them they paid attention to what was important to them, focusing only on what they could do, not once thinking about how something couldn't be done.

> The instruction gained from obstacles is
> invaluable, for it is the making of you,
> not the breaking.

With their right motives, firm resolve, determined persistence, and enthusiastic confidence they had entered the Ground of Good Fortune. Sensing they had done so, they looked about them calmly and immediately saw Opportunity.

'Welcome!' said Opportunity. 'I've been expecting you and knew that you would soon come across me. I am here to take you to Business Incentive Park just a short way ahead, where everyone is expecting you.'

'Who exactly?' asked Chris. 'And how can they be expecting us?'

'Independence, Intrepid and Innovate of course,' answered Opportunity. 'They are the cousins of Intuition and Integrity.'

'Intuition!' said Chris.

'The very same. He evidently knew that you would reach this part of the journey and had, therefore, asked his cousins to expect you. They are looking forward to sharing so much with you over the next couple of days. Afterwards, they will place you on your final road to the Land of Prosperity where Service City lies.'

'So Good Fortune is here at last!' said Chris enthusiastically.

'It is,' replied Opportunity. 'And, for my part, I am very pleased to have the chance to meet you here myself.'

'I am pleased to see you, too, because apparently we just missed each other at Accountability's house. You crossed the path of Redundant, shortly before my arrival, and passed him on to Enthusiasm, who was in the Courtyard. Bad timing on my part, I suppose,' added Chris laughingly.

'But not for Redundant, his timing was just perfect, as was

Enthusiasm's who I usually meet with at most of the places I visit, and with many of the people I help. He's a good friend of mine. I just wish he could be with me more often, particularly when I bump into those people who seem to just want to ignore me. However, it is clear to see that you have spent time with him.'

'Yes, it was because of him that I was able to develop my stamina and firmness of my grasp. The mettle gauntlets he gave to me have become part of me,' said Chris.

Opportunity then turned towards Spontaneity and smiled. 'But I have met with you before, haven't I?'

'You have indeed,' replied the other. 'I came upon you as I was leaving my home town of Frankness and you were kind enough to place me upon Freedom Road.'

'That must surely be a good few years ago now, mustn't it?' asked Opportunity. 'How come it has taken so long for you to get here?'

'I'm afraid that it is more years than I care to remember, but my perception of Superficial Life as a young man led me to believe that I had arrived at Prosperity.'

'And what we perceive we allow to deceive. When our delusion becomes our reality it can be nearly impossible to find ourselves again. So what prompted you to start out again?' enquired Opportunity.

'I happened to look into the mirror longer than usual one morning, I suppose,' said Spontaneity. 'The face looking back at me was like a stranger, though. It was as if I had convinced myself I was someone else and was living the life of another. Then I smiled. I don't know why, but I did. And the more I smiled the more I began to recognise a former friend looking back at me. This friend seemed to ask me if I had any regrets in life. I answered that there were none that couldn't be tempered with time. But then this friend asked if I had any regrets for what I had left undone. It then suddenly came to me to pick

COLIN TURNER

up my path from where I had once abandoned it before it was too late and, well, here I am.'

'Well, you must have succeeded in discovering your old self, or rather young self again. Indeed, it must have been your true self you rediscovered, because I easily recognised you,' said Opportunity. 'As I often say to those I meet, it can never be too late to follow your heart, seek your real fortune and fulfil a meaningful purpose.'

Opportunity turned to Self-Reliance and said, 'Now, I *know* that you and I have met many times before. There have been times when you have chosen to walk with me along a path, and others when you have decided to travel alone, depending on how you have felt. Is that not so?'

'It certainly is so. There have been occasions when I have been so absorbed with another that your company was the last thing I felt I needed,' answered Self-Reliance.

'Ah, it sounds like you're referring to the meeting with my twin brother Adversity,' commented Opportunity. 'Though we tend to travel the same path, he prefers to stay slightly ahead of me and consequently often meets with people before I do.'

'But I had no idea that you were related to that rogue, Adversity?'

'Not many people do, though I have to say he is no rogue. When you get to know him better he's actually a great teacher. Believe it or not, it was he who told me that you had left Prosperity to visit Mediocrity, but he was certain you would return.'

'Yes, but no thanks to him!' Self-Reliance said. 'For it was his influence that made me leave Prosperity the last time.'

'Maybe, but no doubt you have returned stronger than when you previously left. You certainly seem to have disposed of the arrogance and pride that Adversity told me you carried about with you. They were partly the reasons he visited you the last time.'

'You're right about that,' sighed Self-Reliance. 'Indeed, in all honesty, my leaving Prosperity was very much my own fault. I felt that I did not need the help of others, as I thought I could do everything on my own. Now I have learned the importance of channelling my talents in a way that will release my potential, rather than impede it.'

'Yet, what is really good to see is that you have also met up with your friend from years ago, which is what both I, and my brother, hoped for you in the first place. We also hoped that you would see the merit in travelling with these two,' said Opportunity looking at Spontaneity.

Opportunity paused as he looked at the surrounding hills. 'You know my greatest sorrow is that too many people in the world neither achieve what was expected of them, nor enjoy what they themselves hope for. Although the infinite possibilities that exist in the world are great, the probabilities of them ever being utilised are small. What our world needs is like-minded individuals who choose to channel their strengths and talents for a unified and meaningful purpose. Like-minded individuals who choose to build their success on the success of others through bringing opportunities to others and by making the most of their own opportunities. Come on you pilgrims, follow me.'

Business Incentive Park was composed of a fine set of elegant buildings aesthetically placed around excellent facilities. The ambience was one of pleasant harmony, yet our pilgrim could also sense an orderly discipline that was both considerate and resourceful.

Independence, Intrepid and Innovate were clearly delighted to see their visitors and gave them such a welcome that made each feel in turn as though they ruled the world. They eagerly took up the offer to rest and eat well, after their recent adventure at Hesitation Castle, and then rejoined one of their hosts, Innovate, who was still enjoying the company of Opportunity.

'There's nothing quite like being somewhere where you're fully appreciated, is there?' said Opportunity to the three refreshed travellers.

'I must say that it's a new experience for me,' said Chris. 'I don't believe I have ever been as welcomed before by people I have only recently met.'

'Whether you have customers or guests, there can be only one way to welcome them. And that is the right way!' said Innovate. 'What we enjoy doing here is thinking up ways of how we can continuously improve on that *right* way.'

'Many of the creative suggestions made here are recognised in Service City, so it is worth you paying special attention to them,' said Opportunity. 'As for me I must take my leave of you, for the moment, as I am due to meet with some other good friends in Prosperity.'

'We will see you again though, won't we?' asked Spontaneity.

'Now that you have entered the Ground of Good Fortune you can see me whenever you want to. And I can promise you that you'll see even more of me in Prosperity and Service City itself as I have a home there. So bye for now and I'll look forward to seeing you again soon.'

'We'll all look forward to that too,' said Chris as he waved goodbye with his colleagues. Then, turning back to Innovate he said, 'I would love to hear more about your ideas for Service City.'

'First and foremost,' replied Innovate enthusiastically, 'great service requires continuous questioning of existing routines and trying to create something that brings meaningful value. Routine service is something that customers soon take for granted and therefore don't value. Consequently, whatever you do in a routine way will not impress your customers.

'Unwittingly business has a tendency to treat customer relations as just a routine operation. Yet such routines lack emotion and when a service is devoid of emotion customers notice and place no value on it, other than what it has cost them in time or money. So fixed routines take away from service.'

'What is the difference between routine service and Enlightened Service?' asked Chris.

'Over the next few days you will learn most of the secrets of Enlightened Service,' said Innovate. 'And now that you have fully embraced the importance of how your own personal growth is linked with giving better-than-excellent service, you will be able to understand, appreciate and apply what you learn with success. For now, though, let me give you an example of what is believed to be service, yet is simply a routine.

Make the most of opportunities by building your success on the success of others.

'Imagine you take your car in for its service. When you return to collect it you find everything as you expected. The car is ready, the price is about what you expected and the way you are greeted, dealt with and leave is as you expected. A routine inspection begets a routine expectation, but such routine is not actually service. For, whatever is expected cannot be service. Only when there is unexpected benefit and added value can it begin to be deemed service.

'Now, let us imagine that in arranging to take your car in for service, you are unexpectedly offered to have it collected from you, given a loan car and have your own car brought back to you when it is ready. When it is returned your car is in sparkling condition due to having had a full valet and on the seat a small gift has been left with the compliments of the management. Also on the seat is a copy of the work sheet, showing the tasks performed, together with a short handwritten note from the actual mechanic responsible for carrying out the service, saying all is in order and thanking you for your custom. Having been advised by the garage in advance what the service charge will be, you are further pleased to see that what you do have to pay is slightly less. At all times during collection and delivery you are treated with genuine polite friendliness. *That's* service. And what do you do? Do you become a firm ambassador for that garage and tell all your friends? Yes of course you do! But there is something much more important than this. You feel good, you feel safe and you feel valued.'

'Wow! I can't believe that such service could ever exist and even if it did, that people would be nice about providing it,' said Spontaneity.

'The responsibility of business leaders and managers is to educate every one of their people in the importance of putting emotional value into what they do. This they can do by treating their own employees in the same way as their best clients, because they in turn are the business's front line to the customers. And with the dawning of the new customer reign they will have to do this in order to keep their competitive advantage and build their co-operative reputation. Soon, you will not even have to make the call to request service. A computer chip within your car will register when servicing is required, whether it is tyres, exhaust, battery, engine, gearbox of whatever, and inform the garage of your choice directly. Your garage will then have to serve you automatically to maintain its own business reputation, as their chip will also notify the manufacturer of the vehicle as well as other competitors who may be looking for your business.

'Then it will only be the behaviour and attitude of a business that will retain the customer's loyalty. A customer will no longer tolerate being treated as another transaction or a statistic on a survey sheet. Not at all. They will be looking for the emotional value that is genuinely put into building a relationship with them, and the creativity of service. For creativity is closely related to integrity, because developing ways that give more is synonymous with creating trust.

Treating customers like statistics or transactions depersonalises them and the service.

'Trust, of course, is the very foundation of any lasting relationship. When you are building trust it is vital that you deliver what you promise to others, whether they be friends or customers. Indeed, why would you want to treat a customer any different to how you would behave towards a friend anyway? To go further, why would you want to charge your customers for any additional service, when you wouldn't charge a friend? Say you were to buy a car from the garage that I have just spoken about and which actually exists in Service City, and late one night you break your key off in the lock. One call to this garage and their twenty-four-hour service will come and fix it for you, without charging. Now they may charge for something slightly more serious, but their whole customer ethos is based on providing the same kind of service for customers as they would for a good friend. Now, why would they want to do such a thing? Well, in Service City, businesses focus on turning one-time buyers into lifetime customers. Keeping their customers for life by offering free, friendly service for certain peace-of-mind jobs makes better sense to them than paying huge advertising sums to build an image that they hope will win customers.

'The majority of businesses in the world who want to provide good service, however, fall into a difficult trap that is hard to get out of. Because they want to improve their service, as they believe it to be the key to more sales, they have a tendency to promise *too* much. In doing so they raise the expectations of their potential customers who understandably feel let down, even cheated, when delivery does not match up to the promise.'

'Marketing promises are seldom lived up to. And there's nothing worse than getting excited about something only to find that the reality is not as expected,' said Chris.

'But when the product excels the description in the brochure you feel that you have really got something special,' said Spontaneity.

'No business can ever blame the customer for being disappointed, for it can only be the business's own fault,' continued Innovate. 'And it doesn't matter how sincere the business's intentions were, the fact is that if they don't keep their word, they are letting their customer down. To over-promise and under deliver is though, I'm sad to say, just "business as *usual*". Such *normality* is, of course, not conducive to competitive advantage. The only way for businesses to provide good service is to operate *unusually*, which means always delivering whatever is promised or, even better, delivering more.

Customers do not want sincere apologies, they want you to deliver what you promised.

'The only source of competitive advantage, by the way, that a business has is its employees and the service they provide. Therefore all front-line people must be trained to ask themselves a certain question when dealing with customers. And that is: "How would my action look on the front page of tomorrow morning's newspapers?" The most important thing a customer is interested in is did you deliver what you promised you would, for it was because of what you said that prompted me to buy from you. Keeping your word is worth more than all the empathy, the sincere apologies and make-it-up-to-you gifts in the world. Such individual employee ethics, of course, requires that every single employee must have the authority of the chairman when dealing with the customer. And they must always have the authority to resolve their problem. Because good customer service that builds loyalty is just far too important to be passed to some customer relations department. Everybody must be a customer service ambassador for his or her company because that is how the customer perceives it to be anyway.

'People who work in Service City are all ambassadors for their particular business through choice first. And, like any good ambassador, they are absolutely sure about what they do and why they do it. They do not consider that they sell products, they consider themselves as catalysts for turning every one of their one-time customers who chooses to buy from them into lifetime customers. How do they go about this? By doing everything they can that will make the customer feel good about doing business with them. They only consider what *can* be done for the customer, never what *can't* be done.'

'But what if what the customer asks is unreasonable, from a cost point of view?' asked Self-Reliance.

'Ninety-nine per cent of the time the customer requests only small details. Yet, it is the little things that count in service, never the big things. Imagine, for example, purchasing something and then finding when you get it home that it is faulty. You would not be very happy, particularly if you had made a special trip into town to buy it. Upon contacting the business, however, imagine how you would feel if the person who sold you the item called you straight back, apologised for your inconvenience and promised to arrange for another to be delivered to your home that very day. And then phoned you in the evening to make sure you received it. Now, that may cost the business more than the product value, but it would cost much less than the amount required in advertising costs to build a good image to improve customer relations. Because an immediate solution to the problem had been provided, your loyalty to that business would begin to grow. The value of a loyal customer who is more than happy to be an ambassador for a business is immeasurable.

'In that situation the customer was clearly in the right, but is the customer always right?' asked Chris. 'I know that one of my colleagues, Cynical, would argue that the product might have been in good order but that it more than likely stopped working because of improper use by the customer.'

'Those businesses engaged in offering service to others cannot be expected to hide behind the clause *caveat emptor*, let the buyer beware, if they want to develop a competitive advantage. Enlightened Service expects scrupulous honesty, so why should the buyer of a product or service have to be wary? A customer's role is simple. It is to enjoy the benefits of a purchase and not to suffer because of its defects.

'As for being right, well, the customer may not always be right, but as most of them know more about the service that a business provides than the business itself, what they have to say must be valued. So it follows that the customer is always right up to a point. The secret is to decide what that point should be, for the more a business is prepared to give the customer the benefit of the doubt, the more profitable it will be for it in the long run. But let me give you a couple more examples.

It is the little things that make the difference, and a happy customer is a pleasure to deal with, time after time after time.

'I recall being in a shop where several items were on

special offer when I overheard an irate customer demand she be reimbursed for an item she had bought the previous week, which was now selling on offer. Her argument was that if she had waited a week she would have saved the difference anyway. The man she spoke to gave her the small amount of money involved without hesitation. Contented, the woman started to collect some other items that were on offer. The point here is that if you want to keep a customer's business, and encourage them to buy more, then you should give them exactly what they ask for, or even more, without hesitation. If you do anything less you might as well offer them nothing, because you'll have lost their goodwill.'

> Remember, giving better-than-excellent service
> is not a matter of doing customers a favour.
> It's a way of life.

'I suppose the reply could have been "you should have waited a week",' said Chris. 'Certainly the *usual* reaction would be not to reimburse, or at least hesitate in taking any action. *Usually* it is necessary to check with someone more senior and indeed most customer complaints can take weeks before they are processed. And the company *still* thinks they're doing the customer a favour.'

'And think of the time and energy involved in operating a customer relations department that is constrained by a rigid procedure organised by people who do not interact with customers anyway,' replied Innovative. 'On another occasion I was in a dry cleaners when a disgruntled customer was complaining that a suit had been ruined. The suit, which was somewhat old, was so worn in parts that you could almost see through the material. The customer was clearly upset, explained that this was his favourite suit, blamed the cleaning process for being too strong and demanded compensation. The assistant chose not to argue and allowed the customer to vent his anger. The more he was allowed to talk the more he calmed down and began to appreciate the genuine concern that the assistant was displaying. The assistant enquired as to the value of the suit and gave assurance that a fair sum would, of course, be compensated. The customer then started to say that it was probably not all their fault because the suit was old and in a few moments a compensatory sum was agreed and paid.

'I learned from the assistant later that the customer had been coming in for years and they valued his business. The assistant went on to tell me of a situation that had occurred with a customer several weeks before with a dress shirt. The shirt was fairly new but had a tear on the shoulder and a red wine stain on the front. The customer claimed that the shirt had not been torn when he had brought it in and demanded compensation for a sum ten times its value. Such a thing was clearly unfair and the customer was blatantly taking advantage of the good service that was being offered. With great creative service the assistant suggested that she saw no reason why her customer should have the inconvenience of having to get another shirt. So she promised that she would arrange that the same make, style and size would be purchased on his behalf that day and delivered to him, unless he preferred to pick it up later.

> Creative service always beats procedural service
> in the contest to give the best. Use your
> initiative, not the rule book, to solve your
> customers' problems.

'Though the customer was in the wrong, never at any time did the assistant make him feel so. Consequently, his respect for the business could only increase and he would continue to patronise it because it had delivered despite his hidden motives. The main point to remember is that even though some customers may be wrong, or taking advantage, do not show them that you think they are. Simply use creative service to resolve their problem, because though rigid procedural service may allow you to win one time, you will most certainly lose a lifetime customer. The maxim you should follow is, "The only things you never lose, are the things you give away." Thoughtful service costs less than thoughtless service.

'There will, of course, be times when an obnoxious customer is so outrageously unfair and difficult that you will choose to refuse to serve him or her. But though these occasions are rare, too often they seem to form the basis of how to deal with people. In the same way that clinical psychology is based on what makes people unhappy, and never on what makes them happy; it seems that service procedures too often focus on how to handle difficult customers *instead* of how to be friendly with people. Consequently, staff are always preparing themselves for the difficult situations, rather than focusing on how to make the majority of their customer service more effective. We must always try to look for the good in others, even if we are let down, rather than be wary of people because we anticipate that they may be difficult. The one per cent of difficult customers should not form the basis of how the other ninety-nine per cent are treated.

> The best form of advertising costs little and
> works. Better-than-excellent
> service gets personal recommendations
> every time.

'Good customer service is the cheapest, and by far the most effective, form of advertising there is. People will buy from you and keep coming back to you in preference to your competition because of the service they receive. They will constantly reward you through the praises they extol about your business. Such word of mouth marketing is worth a fortune.'

'Consistent delivery of good service must be difficult to achieve though,' said Chris. 'I will never forget the time I was in a restaurant that I had patronised for years. In settling my bill at the end of my meal my credit card was refused. Later it turned out that the bank's computer had prematurely cancelled my card while the new one was still in the post. But the waiter acted as though he had discovered the head of a major fraud gang and his discretion was as subtle as an air raid when he informed me that authorisation for payment had been refused. Phoning the credit card line only exacerbated the situation because their policy was one that the computer must be believed over the integrity of the individual. Although I had been eating there for years, the business had apparently changed hands and there was no one there who knew me. The service was reasonable, sometimes it was quite good, in fact, but to have *good* service most of the time is something entirely different. I would have greatly appreciated the same service to save the acute embarrassment I suffered because of a computer's error.'

'Consistent good service builds goodwill. And it is, of course, the goodwill of a business that can make it *so* valuable,' replied Innovate. 'For example, it does not make you feel good when you have highly recommended a restaurant to your friends only to learn that they did not enjoy it. Even worse is when you accompany your friends and you are treated like a stranger at the establishment you have praised, the service is poor and the food is average. As every business is as strong as its weakest link, the only way to ensure that you deliver consistently is to get your people to always want to go that extra mile. For it is only such action that will turn reasonable service into better-than-excellent service. This requires investment in time, energy and money.

Focus on being friendly with people, instead of relying on service procedures.

'You have already learned that you cannot serve others effectively until you have learned how to serve yourself by being the best you can be through consistent personal development. This follows the principle that leadership and management function more effectively through example, rather than by just procedures and systems. It is pointless to engage in recruiting and training the best people available if you do not live and breathe that which you want your people to do. A business will never achieve better-than-excellent service if management do not *really* believe in it. In believing in it, they will not disagree with the costs that are involved in providing such service. They will also be able to recognise the right people to recruit and train them to be consistent.

'Too often a person "who has seen it all before" will, surprisingly, be put in charge of such people and immediately begin to teach what his or her new recruits must watch out for, based on their own long experience. Then the only thing that is consistent is inconsistent service. Such teachers believe that only by following rules can consistent service be achieved. But for consistent service the only rule to train people with is to tell them to use their own judgement and that if it is necessary to break the rules to please a customer, then they must do so. Development of their judgement of course will come from knowing why they are doing what they are doing, and aligning what is important to them with how they communicate with their customers.'

'If they don't know what they want, then their judgement

will reflect it, of course,' said Self-Reliance. 'It seems that when a person is unsure of who they are and what they want, they become so judgmental that they are unable to use their judgement.'

Use your judgement wisely and always follow your principles. Good judgement develops when you *know* what you are doing, and why.

'Which is why training is so important even if the person being trained may only stay a short period,' said Innovative. 'You will discover in Service City that every front-line person who has first contact with the customer, whether they are receptionists, car park attendants, waiters, shop assistants, operators in hotels or call centre respondents undergoes regular training on friendly customer service. They appraise themselves and are appraised by both colleagues and customers every week. Managers and leaders do the same simply because they see it as setting the right example for their people.'

'But the majority of the appraisals I have ever known outside Service City are done on an annual basis and then the focus is always on what is wrong,' said Chris. 'As for getting their customers to appraise, well that's unheard of. How do you go about doing that?'

'Well, every business in Service City understands that the best way to keep customers is to regularly ask what they like or dislike about the service offered. They don't send or give out time-consuming surveys, because no one likes filling in forms. That's why guarantees are seldom filled in because they are not simple to do. Only companies that are not interested in developing lifetime customers insist on seeing a guarantee before helping you. Being asked just a couple of different questions politely on a regular basis, however, is something that any customer is more than happy to do. But it isn't just front-line people. Everyone asks their particular customers such questions, whether they are internal or external to the business. Questions like:

How well do we deliver what we promise?
How accessible are we when you need to contact us?
How well do we listen to you?
Are we helpful and polite?
Are we doing anything that annoys you?
Do you think we take you for granted?
Do you ever recommend us?

'One receptionist I know phoned her own place of employment out of curiosity to ask if there would be an opening for a job as a receptionist. She was delighted to learn that the business considered their existing receptionist to be one of their most important assets because their customers thought so highly of her. She told me that it was easy to be polite and friendly to her customers because her employers were always polite and friendly to every employee. Businesses that consider their employees to be their customers will consistently seek ways that they can be great in their support service to their employees. They will because they know that the employees' service to their customers will be great accordingly.'

'Because great people give great customer service, which in turn brings great rewards!' said Independence who now joined them. 'So the best employees are always those who have an attitude of responsibility and enjoy a good degree of autonomy in what they do.'

'Employees must be made aware of the importance of their role at the outset. Their training must raise their expectations of what can be achieved. They must appraise themselves regularly and, most importantly, they must be praised for what they do and be well rewarded. Take the receptionist I mentioned earlier, she felt compelled to try and see what her employers truly thought about her work. Although her employers thought she was excellent, treated her in a polite and friendly way she still was not made aware of her important, and much appreciated, role within the employees. Companies that give better-than-excellent service *reward* their people for delivering it. So, it's a case of, raise, appraise and praise your people right and they'll treat your customers right.'

'That's music to my ears,' said Self-Reliance. 'But it strikes me that although many businesses may be very quick to tell their people how special they are to them, their actual recognition and reward seems to be lacking. Even worse, some businesses seem intent on reprimanding their staff when service is *poor*, but say nothing when service is *good*.

Judgmental people are ineffective, effective people use their judgement.

'Often a business that wants long-term growth will hope for better service and greater loyalty, but have a reward system that is linked to speed and total of sales. Strategy is focused on the long-term profits, which is what the former will deliver, whereas bonuses are paid only on the short term, on which the latter is based. Employees, therefore, will focus on short-term budgets instead of long-term growth. The point is that whatever is rewarded gets done. Business will not get from its staff what it may hope for. Business will only get from them what it rewards.'

'So reward the right behaviour and you get the results you want. Fail to reward or to praise the right behaviour and you get the results you don't want,' said Self-Reliance.

'Exactly so,' agreed Independence. 'If you are in business and you are uncertain about how an individual is performing, then look at the sort of rewards they can expect. Because however it is set up will influence their behaviour. A business may hire employees and managers to serve customers face to face, but then "reward" them with a low flat hourly wage and provide little, or no, training in the basics of how to provide good service. The reward, therefore, may as well be interpreted as simply "minding the shop". As for those people who are employed in support of the customer but have no actual contact with them, any customer-linked reward or recognition for effort is non-existent.'

> Front-line positions within a firm are often
> the first customer contact area and of great
> importance. So, why are they usually poorly
> paid with little attention given to training?

'It seems ridiculous that so many businesses give so little training and pay to the front-line positions, yet expect them to give excellent service. Then I suppose when the complaints about poor service flood in, everyone complains that you can't get good people these days,' said Spontaneity.

'So, what exactly needs to be rewarded to ensure that all your employees are customer focused and what must you do to achieve it?' asked Chris.

'First and foremost a customer focused business must have a reward system that expressly rewards its employees – which from now on I will refer to as ambassadors – for rewarding customers by providing excellent service. Secondly, leaders must set the example through their own customer-oriented performance. But before I explain the type of reward system required for your people, always remember that winning and keeping customers depends on rewarding your customers for being customers. The consequences that a customer or potential customer will experience from his, or her, action through contacting a business, or one of its ambassadors, will influence future behaviour. When he or she feels rewarded for their custom, he, or she, will continue as a customer. The less reward, experienced because of off-hand or unvalued behaviour of an ambassador, then the greater the odds that they will discontinue as a customer. He, or she, will become someone else's customer.

How management treats employees is reflected in how loyal customers are.

'Imagine, for example, that you open a new restaurant. Everyone is excited but very nervous about whether everything will be all right. Your ambassadors want to make everything work out well because they also have bills and other living expenses to pay. When the doors first open, therefore, everyone rewards customers for booking and arriving with highly-attentive service, thoughtful behaviour and a friendly welcoming attitude. Within a few months your business is performing really well, with customers returning again and again and new ones pouring in. You start to feel confident because there is so much business to handle and though you may have been a bit abrupt with that last customer, you don't concern yourself too much because there are plenty more coming through the door. But it's at this point that the paradox of success begins to materialise.

'In the ensuing months you are the last to realise that the attention to customers, the quality of service and the intention to perform as well as possible has insidiously declined. With fewer customers and falling sales you keep behind the scenes, busy devising cost-cutting plans, special offers and writing copy for some advertising that someone has suggested you really ought to do. You lay off a couple of former ambassadors, reduce the portions of the meals, rationalising that they were far too generous before, but still the customers don't come back. You blame the economy, the weather and the new competition that has just opened so that you feel that it's not your fault. But the fact remains that it is.

'You stopped rewarding the customers and they voted with their feet. In the beginning you made them feel special, and they liked it and supported your business by coming back again and telling their friends. Then, when business boomed, you began to take them for granted and they withdrew their support. Some even felt cheated. It's that simple. Now perhaps if you had rewarded your ambassadors nothing would have changed and the business would have continued to grow. When your focus changed you unwittingly stopped driving the business, but continued running it into the ground. Your ambassadors simply followed your example.'

'A reward system is certainly the crucial ingredient for a successful business,' said Chris.

Give the right rewards for the right behaviour and enjoy the right results.

'A simple ingredient, yet almost always overlooked,' replied Independence. 'Progress is Man's ability to complicate simplicity and in the chase for it, Man forgets what drives his fellow man to do things. So many people run their homes and businesses on the basis of communicating to their children, spouses, friends, colleagues and employees, or rather I mean ambassadors, when they have done something wrong, or forgotten to attend to something. Management wrapped in hidden agendas and office politics tends to find fault and any form of praise is looked upon as a weakness. Yet, we all know that a short statement of praise makes us double our efforts with a renewed vigour. Simply so that we can receive more of the same.

'With our inherent craving for meaning and purpose, whenever we receive praise for our efforts or rewards for achieving our goals, we feel appreciated, valued and meaningful. Therefore, good business management always starts with clearly communicated expectations, as to the kind of behaviour and results they want. Furthermore, it ensures that absolutely every ambassador has concrete, specific goals. Getting everyone, not just customer-contact ambassadors but *everyone*, to ask themselves, *"What results do I produce and do they benefit the customer?"* will encourage everyone to think about the basics of their job in terms of the customer. Through individual or team meetings everyone should be encouraged and guided into setting their own goals. These goals must be simple and to the point. Each person should only have a couple of goals to focus on at any one time and they should be concisely written for clarity of purpose and commitment. Above all, they must be measurable.'

'Since, if they are not measurable, they cannot be a goal,' put in Innovate. 'Some people will always argue that what they do is just not measurable. Well, when it comes to customer-driven service everything can be measurable. And we can only recognise improvement if something is measurable.'

'And if you can't recognise improvement how can you reward the effort involved?' continued Independence. 'A system manager, for example, may establish that his role is to co-ordinate effective procedures to ensure that all the right products ordered reach the customer right on time and in the right place. His measurable goal would be to reduce the amount of times ambassadors complain about the system by twenty-five per cent, with follow-up goals over a set period to continue to do the same thing. Everyone will benefit, starting with the customer but including the system manager's fellow ambassadors and the business, which can only continue to grow.'

'Goals and measures will only start ambassadors moving in the right direction, of course,' said Innovate. 'You then need specific rewards that will keep them moving. Rewards that they know they will receive at the appropriate time and not some time later.'

'Absolutely! The right rewards for the right behaviour and effort guarantees continuation of the right results,' said Independence. 'Unfortunately, even though some businesses may have goal-setting programmes, when they are not linked in with a specific reward system the programmes fail. And you can imagine what undesired results soon follow with the additional difficulty of low morale.

'Each goal must be linked into a reward when it is achieved. In organisations where it is business as *usual* it is only sales managers and teams that receive commission bonuses. But in linking specific rewards to all goals that have been established, teams and individuals can share in the same benefits. The system manager, for example, will be rewarded for reducing complaints by each twenty-five per cent he achieves. But these rewards are, of course, conditional. For maintained enthusiastic effort on a more regular basis there must be something more.'

'And there is,' said Innovate. 'Many stores in Service City now employ mystery shoppers whose sole purpose is to catch ambassadors doing just the right thing. They are not interested in what he, or she, may be doing incorrectly as that is not their role. They are there as customers and when they see ambassadors performing well they immediately praise the ambassador and give him, or her, a cash reward. Not only that, but the incident is posted to management for special recognition, and for inclusion in any newsletter that may be internally circulated.'

'Wow!' exclaimed Spontaneity. 'That must make the ambassador feel incredible, being praised in front of customers and peers like that. But that's almost unheard of. You would have thought that the mystery shopper would be there to catch the ambassador out and put him, or her, right about where they were going wrong.'

Start with expected goals, continue with unexpected rewards.

'I'm sure companies that operate a business-as-*usual* policy would point out the errors in the belief that people should learn through their mistakes. It is much better to reward ambassadors for doing what you want them to do, instead of continually reprimanding them for doing what you don't want. And, of course, when you do reward them, everyone else makes even more of an effort to achieve their goals and receive "unexpected" rewards. When a manager gives on-the-spot praise, for example, the ambassador feels on top of the world, particularly when praised in front of his peer group. But should the manager castigate him in front of his peers, the ambassador will only feel resentment and he will feel that his day is just full of gloom and doom. Castigation can be done at the right time and in the right place and put in such a way that it does not hurt an individual, but asks why his, or her, behaviour was not in the interests of the team. In other words, positive feedback on improving behaviour is provided. That is another reason why appraisals must be done on a regular basis and not on a ridiculous annual basis.'

'You mention that everyone is always an ambassador, even if they never interact with customers. Do you think that everyone involved in a business will feel that they are an ambassador if what they do is always behind the scenes?' asked Chris.

Employees who have little or no customer
contact should also be encouraged to be
ambassadors. Their input to the atmosphere and
energy of a business is of no lesser
importance. Involve them in the team and show
them they are valued.

'Not *every* salesperson may be an ambassador, but every
ambassador is a customer-focused salesperson because, regardless
of their role, they are an envoy representing the business they
work with,' began Independence. 'Those who are employed
behind the scenes, however, cannot always understand how they
can be salespeople until it is pointed out to them. Let me give
you an example.

'When a new hotel was about to open at Service City
we were invited to give a talk on creative customer service.
Of the four hundred new people involved that made up
housekeeping, engineering, security, reception and operating
employees, banqueting and restaurant, we were told that
there were just five salespeople. In establishing the desired
results, the measured goals and the reward and recognition programme, we suggested that every one of the four
hundred employees, and not just those involved in sales,
should be an ambassador for their hotel by talking about
the benefits it offered to whoever asked. Giving a person
a sense of pride in what they do by giving them a piece
of the action with a reward is a tremendous motivator and
energy builder.

'So, then we suggested that everyone try to get *one* room
booked per year without pressure, but through word of mouth,
and each person would be rewarded with a commission. Well,
the response was phenomenal, everyone knew someone and
all they needed to do was to get one room booked. Maybe

because what was asked of them seemed reasonable, as well as attainable, everyone bought into it. Everyone became an ambassador, with some departments even working together in teams and agreeing to pool their future rewards. Some achieved much more, but every one of the four hundred achieved at least a single occupancy as suggested. They all enjoyed success and the benefits of both reward and recognition. As for the service it became outstanding because, as there was always a guest staying that one colleague had recommended, everyone strove to be the best they could possibly be. Every single employee is now a committed ambassador because they get rewarded for doing what they get paid for anyway, which is looking after the customer.'

'That's where we must stay when we arrive at Service City,' said Chris. 'I can't wait to experience such service! Mind you, that's if they have any room left!'

'Oh don't worry they will be able to accommodate you as they always keep a good percentage of rooms for both regular and new customers. But even if they can't they will arrange something with another hotel as well as a complimentary car to take you there.'

'Gosh, when you make your people ambassadors and reward them accordingly, they must feel like winners,' said Spontaneity.

'Everyone loves to be part of a winning team!' said Intrepid who came in carrying refreshments. 'Give people a piece of the action and they'll think "customer". Give them work they love to do and reward them well for doing it and they'll think "customer". Build in promotion and increased responsibilities, but with the freedom to steer their own goals towards fulfilment, and they'll think "customer". Give them incentives in the form of prizes, whether tickets to the theatre and sport events, dinners or even holidays and they'll think "customer". Maybe more than even you! Make them feel that they're part of something special, part of something fun, yet something that is making a difference in the quality of the lives of others.'

'Even holidays?' said Self-Reliance.

Investing money to support a business is a frequent occurrence. Investing money specifically to treat staff generously is rare. Having the courage to treat staff well will reap the huge reward that they accept without question that the customer comes first.

'Absolutely, because it takes financial courage to treat your people in such a way that they accept without question that the customer must always come first,' replied Intrepid. 'There are even some businesses in Service City that have actually purchased holiday homes for their ambassadors to enjoy using. They consider such an investment as *vital*. Good business acknowledges that rewarding the customer is *everyone's* responsibility and rewarding those who look after the customer is the responsibility of management. But it takes courage to operate your business by always putting customers first and to invest in developing Enlightened Service. When you see all your competitors putting their business before their customers it may cause you to doubt your actions. But the reality is that while they are swimming upstream, vying for restricted space, you are simply going with the current that leads you to the ocean of abundance.'

During the next two days Chris and his colleagues consolidated their understanding of how to give better-than-excellent service. Full of enthusiasm for what lay ahead, they were then taken to the highest point of the Ground of Good Fortune. From there they were able to see quite clearly the final path to the

Land of Prosperity and actually see the tallest towers of Service City itself.

'There before you lies your goal and your future,' said Independence. 'The City where the King, Customer, is a demanding but fair sovereign and advocates that self-government is the best form of government. There you will experience a world of service that is enlightened. A level of co-operative consideration that has long been forgotten in the World of Mediocrity. And you will discover businesses that recognise that their very existence owes itself to Customer. Businesses that will employ ambassadors to work with them, not for them, to fulfil a common purpose, with shared values and common objectives. Ambassadors that have aligned what they do with what they are, out of choice. Taking the ownership of what they have decided needs to be done to fulfil their own personal mission. A mission that recognises that the best way to serve your self is through good service to others. That the best way to learn and grow is to teach and sow. For that which you earn will be based upon what you learn, and the rewards that you reap will be relevant to the service you know and sow.'

Putting your customers first with Enlightened Service will be your best competitive advantage.

'To finally see Prosperity and glimpse Service City makes me forget all the trials and tribulations I have endured along the way. What lies behind me now is nothing compared to what lies before me,' said Chris.

'That which lies before you will make your journey worthwhile, but remember that you have been able to reach it because of what lies within you,' said Intrepid. 'Having the courage of your own convictions, despite what you may come up against, will always provide you with your just reward.'

'I have not seen Prosperity from such a high point before,' said Self-Reliance. 'Tell me, what is that deep cut in the land between here and there?'

'That is the Chasm of Professional Complacency, which you will have to cross with care,' replied Intrepid. 'There is a bridge, though you cannot see it from here. But if you follow the path that we have now directed you upon, you will come directly to it. However, keep your mind on what you are looking for, as there are some that forget and are *still* trying to get across it. You should also be aware that there is a river that borders the city. It is known as the River of Insults. Be careful that at the moment before you reach your goal, you do not get swept away by it, as many good pilgrims have before.'

'But there is a bridge to cross it isn't there?' asked Spontaneity.

'No bridge actually exists,' Intrepid answered. 'You must pass through it, so hold your head high and keep your head above the water.'

'Well, none of us are of faint heart and we have our goal in sight,' said Chris. 'Does the climber give up when his summit is in sight? No, he continues to take one step at a time, but with a renewed vigour. Let's go!'

And thanking their host once more for having shared so much with them, the three companions set off, with Prosperity, and their goal, in sight.

To Be a Pilgrim ...

- Do not treat customers as just another transaction to be processed
- Question routines that may be taken for granted
- Know the importance of putting emotional value in what you do
- Treat your customers like a friend
- Focus on turning one-time buyers into lifetime customers
- Remember that it is the little things that make a difference
- Never show your customer that they may be wrong
- Reward the right behaviour to get the right result
- Be an ambassador as that is how your customer perceives you anyway
- Know that *thoughtful* service costs less than *thoughtless* service
- Do not let 1 per cent of difficult customers influence how you treat your other 99 per cent
- Regularly ask your customers what *they* think of your service
- Set an example through your own customer-focused performance
- Use praise, recognition and reward to motivate your ambassadors
- Know that rewarding the customer is *everyone's* responsibility
- Know that the best way to learn and grow is to teach and sow

Chapter Eight

Arriving at Service City

'That has to have been the best two days since I left the City of Apathy!' exclaimed Chris, walking briskly between his two travelling companions. 'We have learned so many valuable service keys. Yet, isn't it incredible to think that so many businesses clearly operate without such keys and lack a customer service ethos?'

'Yes, because giving better-than-excellent service is actually more simple than giving poor service and certainly more rewarding and profitable for everyone involved,' said Self-Reliance. 'But it's as though the majority of businesses treat both the customer and their employees in a way that is directly opposed to what giving great service requires.'

Avoid making up procedures and rules that interfere with customer relations and restrict your front-line employees.

'It does seem that getting employees to serve a system is the norm, instead of adapting the system to serve the employees who in turn serve the customers,' said Spontaneity. 'Though, until this is pointed out, as it has been to us, how can business be aware of what it is doing to itself? Though customers will

229

know a business for what it really is, the business is often utterly unaware of how they are viewed. Customer service is ultimately about choice. What makes a business successful is the choices that customers make about it, and the way a business chooses to behave towards its customers and ambassadors, communicates with them both and of course encourages them through training and reward.'

'That's right on the button, except that you may not be able to train your customers as you can your ambassadors,' said Chris.

> You may be uncertain as to how your business
> is perceived, but your customers will be able
> to tell you with certainty.

'I don't see why not,' replied Spontaneity. 'After all, the best way to turn a one-time buyer into a lifetime customer is to reward them for being a customer. And where there is reward there must also be training because it follows on. We have learned that the best reward is to be a genuine friend acting with sincere and thoughtful behaviour with attentive understanding to our customer's needs and wants, so that he or she may feel good about the way we serve them. By consistently giving such service we are in effect training them to return to us again and again out of their own choice.'

'Yes, that is true,' said Chris. 'As customers, we do feel much more confident when we have got to know someone in a particular organisation that we are dealing with. Such a friend will take the time to understand our needs and wants. They will give us the time we require and go out of their way for us. They will make us feel valued and special.'

'And such a friend is developed in business through thought-ful attentive service,' put in Self-Reliance. 'I can't wait to experience such friendly service ambassadors who understand success in customer service is founded on personal commitment to improvement, alignment to a meaningful mission, enthusiasm, innovation and a passion to bring the very best to their customer.'

'Ridiculous!' exclaimed Analysis who had just appeared. 'Absolutely ludicrous! The very idea of allowing a customer's likes and dislikes to enter into the process of making business decisions is ludicrous, and goes against the rational backbone and logical framework that makes business what it is! I suggest you empty your head of such ridiculous notions if you ever hope to cross this rift before you.'

'We believe that the *key* to success is to be a product of company policy,' added Paralysis who was travelling with Analysis. 'Not to express your own feelings and thoughts, or listen to those of your customer. Customers are much more amenable and secure, let me tell you, when they are told what to do.'

Appearing suddenly from a sharp turn in the path as they had, the team of Analysis Paralysis had taken Chris and his companions by surprise. Just slightly beyond the path plunged a huge chasm. It was not possible to see clearly the other side but Chris could just make out a small footbridge visible in the distance.

'And when my colleague says "key", he's right because we know all there is to know about customer service, business acumen and scientific management,' said Analysis. 'There isn't anything that we haven't either investigated or written a procedural report on. And there's nothing we have not measured in the form of efficient performance appraisals and total quality management either. So don't talk to us about the necessity for emotional input, empathy or reliable care because we're not interested. We've heard it all before and there's no reason or logic to it.'

'And if there's no logic to it then it won't work!' added Paralysis.

'Then why are you skulking around jumping out at people instead of living it up in Prosperity across from here?' demanded Chris confidently.

'Skulking around! Jumping out!' said Analysis. 'I'm afraid you are mistaken! We have no reason to skulk or jump out, as we know every inch of this side we are on. Every inch, let me tell you. It's people like you who disturb the peace with your ideas of letting systems serve people instead of employees serving the system. And, let me tell you, that we can transverse this rift before us whenever we want to. It's just that on examination of the bridge required to reach Prosperity it is clear that its thickness will not support its length. As good citizens we have submitted our report and are waiting here for something to be done. It would be illogical to do otherwise.'

'Except we have not actually submitted our report yet,' corrected Paralysis. 'Because there are still a few points that we have to compile for its conclusion.'

'Which makes perfect sense but as soon as it is done, and we have both signed it off, it will be submitted,' returned Analysis.

'I've heard of you,' said Chris. 'You were a pupil of Discipline once, and a very precise one at that, though one that enjoyed the deliberation of an obstacle in preference to actually surmounting it. And you,' added Chris looking at Paralysis, 'were a fine pupil of Persistence, but your insistence on perfection has always stopped you from reaching where you are going.'

Being pedantic impedes your growth.

'We are not the slightest bit concerned about what you have

232

or haven't heard about us,' replied Analysis. 'Last year we both appraised each other in detail and are pleased with how we are doing, thank you very much.'

'Absolutely,' added Paralysis. 'But the real point is we know why *we* are here. We consider it our duty to ensure that errant business pilgrims have really examined why they are on this road in the first place. This is not a path for inspired, time-wasting aspirants, you know.'

'Under what authority do you block our way as you do?' enquired Chris. 'We are on this path because we have earned our passage through knowing what we stand for, and developing a strategy and customer ethos. And if it is a toll you are after then "let *me* tell *you*" that our willingness to learn, understand and apply enlightened service is all that is required to cross this bridge. A bridge I might add that I and my friends are prepared to trust in with regard to its strength and direction.'

'Strong confident words for one who has not yet displayed what you profess to be enlightened service,' said Analysis. 'Although I do not agree, you no doubt consider that customer relations are no different to human relations. So I put it to you that our authority comes from the compilation of our own procedural report wherein we state that people who profess to walk their talk should be tested to the point of proof. Let us therefore imagine that I am your customer wishing to cross this bridge that you are so confident of. Are you prepared to submit to my questions? And, if you are, are you then prepared to accept the consequence of not crossing over should my assessment of your service be not acceptable? Indeed, shall we say accept even the consequence of others crossing in your place?'

For a moment Chris's thoughts flew back to Discipline's words about how the Analysis–Paralysis duo perceived their duty as one of confronting and questioning pilgrims to see if they should really continue forward or turn back. He also remembered the danger of dealing with people with ulterior motives. But the fact was that he knew his own motives and was therefore clearly able to see the motives of these two before him. They were both unable to find a way across themselves because they were so habitually immersed in procedural and policy minutiae. As such they were out to take the place of Chris and his companions through stealing *their* confidence and casting doubt over their undertaking. What did Intrepid say? Something about keeping your mind on what you are looking for, as there are those still trying to get across. 'Well,' he thought, 'I bet these two are still looking for a way, even though they seem more intent on stopping others.' Above all, though, he must have the courage of his convictions. For, there was no way that he was going to allow himself, or his friends for that matter, to be tricked, distracted, convinced, cajoled or even persuaded from the path they had chosen.

'I see no reason to be tested on the truth which exists in my heart,' replied Chris. 'Though I am prepared to submit to any questions that you might pose on the basis that when I answer correctly, you will straight away stop confronting future pilgrims on this path.'

'But that is what I do,' said Analysis innocently. 'For how else can I myself walk my talk? After all, is it not right that we should have the courage to stick to our convictions?'

'With your capacity for examination, would it not be more desirable to find out why customers are loyal to a business instead of why it is important for an employee to become a product of company policy?'

'But we have already agreed that you will submit to *my* questions, not I to yours. So your question is academic,' replied Analysis.

'Now then,' he added, 'answer me this. What is the established system for delivering business success?'

Systems alone cannot deliver success, it is achieved through the desire of the system makers to be successful.

When no one appeared to have any reply Chris continued to talk and began to list much of what he had learned to them, slowly and clearly.

'Remember, systems in themselves do not deliver success – it is the system makers that *must* have the desire to achieve it.

'So, one. This demands embarking on your own journey and meeting with Intuition!

'Two. Follow your heart!

'Three. Evaluate your motives!

'Four. Accept personal accountability!

'Five. Release your burden!

'Six. Develop a charter!

'Seven. Overcome insecurity!

'Eight. Endure the dark night of the soul!

'Nine. Pass through superficial life!

'Ten. Commit to purposeful leadership and team direction!

'Eleven. Embrace opportunity!

'Twelve. Learn through self-government, courage and creativity!

'Then and only then you will have the understanding of how to give better-than-excellent service!'

Both Self-Reliance and Spontaneity cheered Chris, even though they were being glared at by Paralysis.

'Would you agree that in compliance with scientific evidence of management practices it is better for business to predict what products will sell, than know what customers will buy?' asked Analysis.

'I believe that all the scientific management in the world

pales into insignificance in comparison to understanding the needs, wants, likes and dislikes of a customer. Such a thing can only be achieved through attentive, friendly, reliable service, not through artificial procedures.'

'So, you believe that subjective emotions drive success with customers, rather than rational objectivity?' asked Analysis.

'Though goals and rewards must be measured, scientific management seeks to measure what people do, rather than what they achieve. Activity is therefore deemed more important than productivity. Thus, the person who sees ten customers in a day is considered more worthy than the person who takes time with just five. Yet, the latter is more inclined to develop the relations that the long-term strategy of a business hopes for. We are not machines following some programme which rationalises that a certain number of transactions must be dealt with in a certain way and in a certain period. Our ability to be influenced by our emotions and feelings makes us the people that we are and helps us to achieve the things we do.

'The philosophy of pursuing rational objectivity in order to reach business decisions frowns upon the use of emotion, yet after all our massaging of figures and rationalisation of surveys we return to discover that our original feeling for some thing was right. Thus it is emotion that drives a business, a passionate emotion emanating from the belief and commitment of those driving it. People neither do what they do, nor buy what they buy because of logic. They do and buy because of how they feel, or how it makes them feel, and then apply rational thinking to justify what they do, or what they buy. The truth is that if people do not believe in you, it's because you don't believe in yourself. True belief comes from how you feel about what you do, why you do it and how important it is to you. Such belief cannot be based on rational objectivity.'

'Hmmm, although I applaud your rhetoric, I cannot agree

with either of your answers,' said Analysis. 'For to do so would demand too much of a change in my thinking. However, do not forget that I am your customer in this debate. Therefore, following your commitment to Enlightened Service, I must be right. So I win!'

'You win nothing,' returned Chris. 'For you have not asked any service of me other than question my beliefs and integrity. Neither of those I compromised, nor did I offer you a disservice by misguiding you. Your test was to see if I would walk my talk. Well, for words to match deeds, allow my very commitment to cross this bridge, that you are so convinced is unsafe, to be the proof you require.'

'And we're with him,' added Self-Reliance and Spontaneity in unison.

'Then you're crazy and deserve to fall into Professional Complacency like so many have before you who became overconfident in themselves,' scoffed Analysis. 'When you fall from that bridge you will meet many businesses that appear to be profitable in spite of themselves. But really they are going nowhere, believing they no longer have to try. Come take a look.'

As his companions went to the edge and Analysis pointed down into the depths of abyss, Chris remembered the significance of Intrepid's words.

'Don't look down!' he shouted. 'We must keep our minds on what we are looking for and not on what others have chosen to do.' With that Chris stepped on the bridge and began to walk confidently across. Both Self-Reliance and Spontaneity followed his lead and within a few moments found themselves in a thick mist.

'It must be coming up from below,' said Spontaneity. 'It's almost impossible to see.'

'We don't have to see with our *eyes*,' answered Chris. 'Just keep our minds on what we want.'

After what seemed an eternity of focused concentration, they made step by step progress and emerged in the bright sunlight of Prosperity.

'Imagine falling into the Chasm of Professional Complacency,' said Self-Reliance. 'For a business to enjoy Good Fortune and then become its own impediment to continuing on to Prosperity seems such a waste of potential.'

'To fall into such a place reminds me of living a Superficial life,' answered Spontaneity. 'How easy it is when you believe you are successful, market leaders and ahead of your competitors, to lose sight of your *raison d'être* and allow yourself to become the issue, instead of the vision.'

'Such businesses become so comfortable believing their own propaganda about how successful they are in comparison to others that they no longer consider it necessary to try, and end up being lost in the midst of their own importance,' said Chris. 'Is it any wonder that the majority of businesses do not survive one generation when they view the future as merely an extension of the past? Yet success is not about comparing ourselves in relation to what others have either done or not done. Success can only be measured in relation to what we ourselves are capable of.'

'And all that businesses need to do is remind themselves why they are in business and what is important to them,' added Self-Reliance. 'Such reminders, however, are either ignored or merely paid lip-service. Indeed, ask people why they are doing the work that they are and the majority will answer "to make money of course!" In seeking to chase their pension, rather than their passion, they get by, rather than fulfil themselves. Paid work, chosen work and visionary work can be likened to asking three masons working on the same stone what they are doing. The first, who is both disinterested and bored, replies that the very fact he is sweating in the sun chipping away at some stone clearly shows he is working for money. The second satisfyingly and enthusiastically replies that he is carving a statue, which is bringing the sculptor out in him that he always wanted to be. The third replies with a passion in his eyes and a sense of purposeful pride in his heart. For he is building a magnificent cathedral, which though it may not be completed in his lifetime, will be looked upon in awe by generations to come.'

'To be a part of something that you consider has a true goal, instead of seeing it just as a job, is the key to living a rewarding life. For to be involved in something worthwhile provides meaning and purpose in itself.'

> Make your job rewarding by being part of a cause that makes a difference. Personal involvement brings a sense of purpose into life.

Chris paused as he strained his eyes to look at two travellers who had now come into view. 'But look, I'm sure I recognise one of those people.'

The three pilgrims quickened their pace and soon caught up with the two ahead of them. Chris was delighted to see that it was Entrepreneur, who having escaped from Superficial with the help of his friend, Influence, was now on his way to Deal, a stock-market town close by.

'So, you have made it to Prosperity at last,' said Entrepreneur after the four had greeted each other. 'I'm glad to be back here myself after my short experience of Superficial life. When my good friend Influence came looking for me he reminded me to get on with what I was good at, rather than waiting around for something to happen.'

'Then what a fortunate man you are to have such a good friend,' said Chris.

'Don't I know it,' replied Entrepreneur.

'I simply reminded you to impress upon others what your strengths and abilities are, so that they would realise it was pointless to hold you back,' put in Influence. 'It would have done no good at all to persuade your captors to let you go through forceful methods, or conditional plea-bargaining.'

'Like saying to a customer, if you do not buy this today, you're going to lose out to someone else,' said Chris.

'Yes, only in this case with all the trumped-up charges, the argument was, if you say yes to us we'll give you a reward,' replied Influence. 'The "yes" of course, was to accept that their "Brand Image" was the very best available, so that we must always buy from them and use their service. Superficial people, of course, believe that advertising campaigns are the only way to build brand image. They won't accept that customers buy because of the feel-good factor of purchasing a particular product or service that fulfils what it promises, and continues to always do so. It would have been useless to argue against such fixed thinking so we suggested that we have the opportunity to try all their products and services so that we could tell the world about them.'

'And they liked the idea,' added Entrepreneur. 'So they released me immediately and allowed us to shop at ease. This time, of course, I did not advocate my own service in preference to their own. I was careful to keep my own counsel but at the first opportunity I voted with my feet and we left the awful place. But you can be sure that I will keep my word. For the whole world must be made aware of such awful service!'

'The service challenge for business must be to make each contact with every customer such a positive experience that the customer perceives the business as excellent. This is critical because customers do not buy because of the quality or excellence of a product or service. They buy because of the quality, or excellence, that they *perceive*. And it is their perceptions that will cause them to both purchase a product and recommend the business to friends and colleagues,' said Influence.

For the customer to perceive a business as excellent, every contact must create a positive experience.

'Customers must feel good about dealing with a business to continue to do so,' said Chris. 'No one wants to deal with someone they don't like. Particularly when sharing our desires with a business that promises to fulfil them for us, and then lets us down.'

'Often customers, of course, are reluctant to share their desires in case they are ridiculed because of their lack of knowledge, or are embarrassed for asking a stupid question,' said Self-Reliance. 'Which is why it is so critical that the front-line ambassador seeks to develop an empathy with a customer. The more they get to know a customer, the more they will be able to ensure that the experience the customer perceives will be outstanding.'

'And the greater the empathy, the greater the understanding of the customer. I believe that causing a customer to feel better about dealing with you because of how you deal with the customer is the best,' Influence said. 'It's developing the small tendencies that are important. Like greeting a person with a warm smile and then using their name on subsequent occasions.'

'Which reminds me, we must make our way to Deal for we are meeting with Opportunity there,' said Entrepreneur. 'Why don't you join us?'

'Perhaps another time, thanks. Right now, and I believe I speak for my colleagues, we are determined to make Service City our next stop,' answered Chris.

'And I am sure you will want to make it your last stop when you experience it,' said Entrepreneur. 'Always remember to return more than you receive and to consider yourself self-employed in everything you do — even if you work with another. Because when you think in such a way you bring out the very best in yourself.'

'And you bring the best out in others,' added Influence. 'For the best entrepreneurs must have management skills and the best managers must think like an entrepreneur. Such leaders are neither timid nor cavalier at whatever they do. They simply do things that they know to be right, have to be done and are in line with their vision.'

'There's certainly nothing quite like a vision to keep a person on track,' said Chris. 'One of the most important things my travels have taught me is that you must know where you are going. Otherwise, how will you recognise it when you get there? And to keep your mind on where you are going and why.'

'Or, you end up exactly at the place you always dreaded that you might end up, such as imprisoned in Superficial life listening to Contempt!' laughed Self-Reliance.

> To succeed with customer-focused service, managers must think like entrepreneurs, while entrepreneurs must have management skills.

Having taken their leave of Entrepreneur and Influence the three pilgrims continued through Prosperity. On the way they first met with Encouragement who confirmed that they were almost there.

'Continue taking one step at a time and the success of your journey will be assured,' he said. 'Without the obstacles that you have had to overcome you would feel little satisfaction in reaching Prosperity.'

'Now that we are here whatever complaints we might have had are forgotten,' said Chris.

'Of course, but complaints are not a bad thing when they are viewed as a sign that something is not quite right. When the body has a complaint, for example, it indicates that health is suffering. Indeed the citizens of Service City consider a complaint as an opportunity to build relationships. In treating co-workers as customers, for example, a business there will review its whole customer ethos if it considers that its own people may have cause to complain about anything. For such a business understands that demotivated ambassadors will find it hard to be motivated in what they do.'

'I understand that the River of Insults lies just before Service City,' said Spontaneity. 'Does everyone have to cross it each time they enter?'

'Everyone does, but it gets easier each time simply because you become impervious to the water. Someone who is new to Prosperity and wants to enter the City is more prone to having their thinking tested than another who knows what to expect. For, whatever we expect is right. If you think you can't do something, then you are as right as if you think you can. For whatever outcome you believe will happen, you manifest for yourself. The important factor is do not think of reasons why something can't be done, just find a way to do it. Above all, do not panic no matter what, even if your head goes under. Just think to yourself that you will never give up and keep trying until you win through. Remember this though. Whatever someone thinks of you is none of your business. You cannot get inside their mind and change their thinking. Only they can do that to themselves. What's important is what you think of yourself, for this is what will ultimately determine your success. Believe you will succeed.'

*   *   *

Next they met with Tolerance who, despite being absorbed in what he was doing, took the time to greet and talk with them.

'You will learn that one of the key factors of success in Service City is the ability to get on with other people. To do so, it is important to like people. But you cannot like people if you do not like yourself because then you will be impatient with yourself and thus be impatient with others.

'We cannot communicate more than what we are. If we are impatient for someone to make a decision, then that is what we will communicate, even without words. Thus the customer knows when the person they are speaking to, either on the phone or face to face, is taking the time they are due, or merely rushing them. Human error exists and mistakes happen, but those ambassadors who feel they are appreciated, valued and trusted do so because they know that their employers patiently take the time to explain what is required so that the mistake is not repeated. To reprimand without explanation or understanding is not in the interests of training the ambassador, the interests of the customer nor the growth and profitability of the business. People like to know that decisions are fairly made. In that way they can be open about their mistakes and feel accountable for what they do.'

After Tolerance they met with Reliability who informed them that news of their imminent arrival had already reached the city.

'Everyone has heard of you because you are doing what you have said you will do right from the start. Consistent performance is what the King, Customer, desires in business more than anything else. And consistent, one hundred per cent, high-level performance is what every business in the city strives for. It is considered the essential competitive advantage for any business seeking to set the global service standard of excellence within their industry.

'In that way, the Customer can enjoy zero defects within the realm. Providing better-than-excellent service makes the difference between real champions and the also-rans. So, when you consider that the number of your repeat customers is in direct proportion to the consistency of your service, always ensure that you never let people down. A consistently *unreliable* friend cannot be a true friend by definition. If you cannot rely on your friends, who can you rely on? To be a friend to Customer you must be reliable for it is the best way to build a trusting relationship.'

> Business seeking to set the global service standard of excellence within its industry, must provide consistent, one hundred per cent, high-level performance.

Finally, they met with Kindness who, full of praise for how they had overcome all of their challenges in order to arrive where they were now, took the opportunity to share with them how consideration will beget reward.

'Under the Law of Contract, there must be a form of consideration agreed between the parties for it to be binding. Indeed, without such a consideration specific performance of the contract can not be enforced. Consideration is the key that makes it meaningful. But take any interaction between two people, be it husband and wife, doctor and patient or customer and business. Without consideration, what meaning has the relationship? None at all. When people are inconsiderate towards each other there is always a consequence. And you can be sure that pain will be involved.

'Being considerate to others is more than treating them as you would like to be treated. It means more than feeling sympathy for their problems and more than wanting to make them feel good. It involves the sincere empathy of putting yourself in their shoes, yet making them feel good because you are seeing things from a slightly different perspective. Because you are *not* in their shoes. It is with such clear thinking that you are able to assist them with what they want and provide the solution that will make a difference. Choosing to serve another willingly is being considerate. And such consideration brings greater reward than you would expect.

'The Law of Service promises that you will always be rewarded in life, in exact proportion to the value of your service to others. The Law of Enlightened Service, however, promises that you will always receive in life greater-than-expected rewards in consideration for how you have treated others. Such rewards may not always come from where you thought, or at the time you hoped. But they will *always* come and will *always* be greater than expected. Enlightened means to be at one with the light, with light being the metaphor often used to convey the level of our conscious awareness. As we become aware of how we can serve ourselves through better-than-excellent service it's as though we emerge from darkness. "Let there be light" is apt as the central image of creation. For it is also the epitome of how our own awareness makes us grow.' The awareness that the 'I' is best developed through serving the 'we'.

> Greater-than-expected rewards always come from treating others as you would like to be treated.

Shortly after our pilgrims' four encounters, which each caused them to grow in Prosperity, they saw in the distance the shining city of Service, bathed in the afternoon sunshine. Two enormous towers seemed to rise almost to the sky and although the city walls were high the central gate looked inviting. Across their path, however, lay a fast rushing river.

'That must be the River of Insults and our final obstacle,' said Chris. 'We just have to cross it and we have reached our destination.'

'It looks deeper than I imagined,' said Spontaneity.

'Remember that we must believe we will succeed in order to cross it,' said Chris. 'Our imagination is at our disposal to find the way towards our dreams. It is not there for our disposal of them. It can't be that deep, so long as we keep our heads up high, and it is certainly not wide. Come on, we'll be across it in no time at all.'

Almost as soon as they entered the water, each pilgrim began to have some serious doubts about holding their own against the strong current.

'Come on, you good-for-nothing laggard!' Self-Reliance thought he heard Chris shout scornfully.

'What did you say?' he shouted back, but Chris did not hear over the shout that he believed he heard Spontaneity make.

'Your worthless vision will kill us all, you fool!'

'What?' shouted Chris.

'You're nothing but a nuisance with all your stupid ideas that no one's interested in!' Spontaneity could have sworn Chris shouted in response to his cry for help when he lost his footing.

'Let him drown, that's all he's good for!' he heard Self-Reliance yell at him as he just managed to keep his head above water.

'Why are you saying such cruel things?' Spontaneity spluttered.

Seeing his friend sink under, Chris turned back and drew his sword of Steadfastness. Seeing this action Spontaneity panicked, thinking that Chris was out to harm him for some reason.

Chris plunged his sword into the riverbed to anchor himself as he reached for Spontaneity. Seeing Chris's action, Self-Reliance realised that the River of Insults was somehow distorting their shouts.

'This water is affecting our very thinking,' he thought to himself. 'Above all we must not panic, for we will win through. We will not be halted at the moment of our achievement because of meaningless insults.'

Reaching his fellow pilgrims he linked arms with them and with determined faces they inched their way to the other side. As they did so the noise abated until all that could be heard were affronted whisperings.

'That was awful!' cried Spontaneity. 'The things that I, at first, believed you two were shouting at me filled me so much with fright that I almost drowned!'

'What a current of abuse. It was trying to make us fall even though we are so close to what we have worked so hard for,' said Chris. 'What we allow ourselves to listen to can be our very undoing!'

'Learning to be impervious to those who are intent on pouring scorn on our endeavours is one thing,' said Self-Reliance. 'But how alarming to consider how quickly we began to misunderstand each other!'

'I believe that reaching our destination can only ever be our beginning. The building of trust and sincere friendship is a continuous process. With our minds so full of wrong conditioning about our fellow man, how could it be otherwise? Until, of course, we learn to fully trust ourselves and have confidence in our own thinking. For trustworthiness in the individual can be the only factor that builds trust towards others. In developing our own trustworthiness we will replace the habit of looking for slights in what others say when we feel vulnerable. And when another is clear about their trust in you, it is the true nature of Man to honour it. Listening to insults can only mean that we are hoping to hear some endorsement for what we do. Such a thing must be taken as an indication that we are suffering from low self-esteem and are not fully confident in our endeavours.'

'Whereas constructive criticism can be a useful guidance, insults are spawned from jealousy, envy, anger and distrust,' said Self-Reliance. 'To harbour such emotions is the same as keeping rotting food in the refrigerator, believing that it is a waste to throw it out.'

'There is one good thing though,' said Spontaneity having got his breath back. 'I suppose that the day people stop insulting you, or saying things about you behind your back, is the day you've stopped growing!'

'Well, it's certainly true that successful mainstream businesses are always current news!' laughed Self-Reliance.

As they walked up the hill from the bank towards the city they saw the gatekeeper, Trustee, come out to meet them.

'Welcome!' he said smiling warmly. 'It's great to see that you have arrived. I am sure that you will want to enter our beautiful city without delay having crossed that river down there. It was good to watch you get across in no time at all. And the good news is that now you know what to expect, next time when you seek to do things differently and for the best, you will experience no difficulty at all. Some pilgrims, I'm afraid, make a harder time of it and even forget their reason for having travelled here in the first place.'

Realising that Trustee was asking, in a polite way, to see his charter Chris searched inside his breast pocket for it. 'I stand to deliver and my friends are with me,' said Chris as he held his charter out.

'What you are is so clear for me to see that I have no need of proof,' said Trustee. 'That charter is yours to remind *you* about what you stand for. But when you walk your talk, you have no need to declare it to the world. Because the world can see it for itself and knows it. You are free to enter Service City, for you have already paid the price of success. And you have paid it in advance, which is the only way it can be bought.'

Reaching what had been such an important goal for him left Chris lost for words. Deep down he had a confidence such as he had not experienced before. It was coupled with a sense of accomplishment for having arrived at his destination, despite his trials and tribulations. He believed that everything he had gone through had been worth it because the value of his self-worth had risen immensely. He had done it! He would now enjoy the rewards of his journey but at the same time he would begin to devise new goals and new plans, all within the framework of his mission. For the meaning of true success was not where you were at, but in which direction you are going. Success is the *continuous* accomplishment of planned objectives that are worthwhile to the individual. Success itself does not lie in the achievement of the goal, although that is what the World of Mediocrity would consider success. Instead it lies in the journey towards the goal. Success is a journey. It is the result of a change in thinking, attitudes and new habits acquired during that journey. True success is having belief in yourself and accepting that it is just another name for your unlimited power. 'Yes,' Chris said as he voiced his thoughts. 'True success bears no relation to the person you are before you embark upon its journey. It's your potential to be the person you can become and *will* become when you make a definite resolution *to be a pilgrim.'*

As the world can clearly see if you are walking
your talk, you have no need to declare it.

After entering the city, Chris and his friends were met by two courtiers of the King, Care and Respond who took them to the very same hotel that Independence had recommended. On the way there Care and Respond volunteered details about the service ethos that was prevalent in the city and sought-after by King Customer.

'Delighting Customer is considered the only strategy that works here,' said Care. 'So all business leaders ensure that both their vision of what they stand for and strategy for delivering it are articulated to all of their ambassadors. Customer doesn't care how much you know, until he knows how much you care, so it is important that your service strategy is clear and concise, well understood and internalised by everyone in the business. Such a strategy is firmly adhered to because it is considered that a policy of continually launching new slogans to entice new customers will be ignored. Once a company knows what it stands for, they must keep to it and only focus on backing it up with performance.

'Peace of mind is what Customer wants and he is both willing to pay for it and return to ambassadors and businesses that have clearly indicated by their actions that they have his best interests at heart,' said Respond. 'He wants security, integrity and the assurance that if there is a problem it will be handled at no extra cost. He wants credible service, not hidden agendas or charges, get-out clauses and hard sell methods. If he chooses to buy products he wants them to do what they promise and be reliably safe. With any professional services, such as medical, legal or financial, he wants them to be free from liability, appropriate for him and kept confidential. He also wants to be kept informed as to whether he will have to wait for what he wants and if so for how long.

'Take the time that his television stopped working one evening as an example. He called the service number, which he had been given when he bought it, and was informed that they would send someone out that very evening. Within ten minutes he was called back and informed that an engineer would be with him within the hour. The friendly but courteous engineer came within the hour. Though the engineer had brought with him a free loan TV set in the event that he was not able to repair his customer's, he did manage to get the TV working. Although the engineer did not request it and offered to send an account, Customer chose to settle his payment then and there, after which the engineer departed. An hour later the service department called back to make sure everything was back to normal for Customer. A few days later Customer received a letter thanking him for his business, appreciating his advance settlement but enclosing a form to open an account and a sticky label to place on the back of the set, should Customer so choose to use the service, for future convenience.'

'Excellent! At every occasion Customer was kept well informed!' said Chris. 'After all, no one likes to wait, particularly when someone has promised that they will do something.'

'And the service department did not take Customer for granted either,' said Spontaneity. 'They phoned to check and then even wrote to thank him for his patronage.'

'Which is why Customer will always continue to use them, so long as they do not become complacent and take the view that treating him any less than they have previously done will not matter,' replied Respond. 'Because it will. After all, any customer would be offended if their patronage was taken for granted and they became just another transaction.'

'But you are talking about the King of the city,' said Self-Reliance. 'Businesses will be obliged to treat him with the utmost respect because he is royalty. So I must ask, is everyone treated in the same way?'

'Every customer is treated like royalty, if you like, without exception,' said Respond. 'Businesses here never discriminate because of titles or social status. Everyone is made to feel special because, as far as every one of us is concerned, each one of us is the most important person alive, aren't we?

'But let me tell you a story about when Customer first came here, long before there was a city. Years ago there was just a small town here populated by all the well-to-do people living in Prosperity. One of the shops was a large well-established patisserie. The shop only sold expensive, high-quality products and the customers were largely upper-class families in the town. One day a poor scruffy-looking youth entered the shop and asked for one of the delicious-looking cakes that was in the window. It was very unusual for such a bedraggled person to shop in such a proud establishment, and the young assistant who waited on him was uncertain at first how he ought to respond to his request. Finally, the assistant wrapped up the cake. When he was about to hand it over, however, the owner of the shop appeared and stopped him. "Just a moment," he said, "let me attend to that." The owner, who had created the cake, took the package from the assistant and presented it to the customer. As he received the money from the scruffy man, he thanked him with very courteous words and then went round the counter to politely open the door for him.

'Puzzled and confused, the young assistant asked the owner, "Sir, why did you wait on him yourself? You've never done that before. It's always one of us, or the cashier, who handles the sales."

'The owner nodded and replied, "That's right, but that particular customer was special. We should be truly grateful that he came in today."

'"But what's so special about him, sir?" the young assistant asked.

'"Our regular customers are all well-to-do people. There's

nothing unusual about them buying our products. But that young man wanted that cake so badly that he probably spent everything he had just to buy it. Shouldn't we be grateful to such a customer? That's why I decided to serve him myself. As a businessman, nothing pleases me more than his kind of patronage. It was as though he was giving himself a reward for something and he chose my product and service to fulfil it."

'You see, I was that young assistant,' said Respond. 'And that day I learned an invaluable lesson on what business is all about. The confectioner knew the real joy of business. For him, the customer's worth did not depend on his social status or wealth or even the size of his purchase. Both a business and its ambassadors' greatest pleasure are surely in being able to satisfy customer's needs, and they ought to be grateful for every opportunity to do so.

'As for the scruffy youth, I learned later that it was Customer himself and he had indeed been rewarding himself for having chosen to leave mediocrity behind, seek his fortune through the release of his potential and arrive here. It was also the last few coins he had in the world and he considered rewarding himself for his personal effort as vital for his future success. I remember he told me much later that, "If we cannot even praise ourselves for the achievement of our goals, then what little value do we assign to ourselves? For if we do not believe that what is important to us warrants reward, then in our own eyes we may as well be worthless." '

Respond paused before adding, 'That, of course, was quite a few years ago now, but it was because of Customer's experience at the patisserie that he resolved to become a leading advocate of better-than-excellent service. He created a service ethos that would help business achieve greater-than-expected rewards for what they did. He realised that many businesses struggled with the paradox of providing service while making money at the same time. After all, the usual excuse in business for doing without it is that service is a costly exercise. But the reality is that greater profitable reward is a result of providing an improved service.

'It is the duty of business, of course, to make a profit. Otherwise a business cannot be in business, and it is being either philanthropic or just indulging in a hobby. Business must furthermore fulfil needs and wants, likes and dislikes. Because, similarly, any business that doesn't cannot be termed a business. But when service in relation to fulfilling needs and wants is the main focus, with proper care paid to overheads and profit margins, ambassadors develop the attitude that they are helping customers by what they do. In so doing they open the way to personal growth, for at work you produce something, but in service you *become* someone.

'This is acknowledging that the primary purpose of business is to provide service. Profit and reward is simply the applause you get for satisfying customer needs and wants. So if a business desires more applause it simply has to improve its service performance. In doing so it is creating a fulfilling work environment for its ambassadors and a welcoming, reliable and credible establishment for its customers.'

'And generating a genuine desire for full involvement and enthusiastic participation with all ambassadors is the key to developing and applying a service ethos effectively. Because such involvement releases the enormous, yet usually untapped potential, within a business,' added Care.

Arriving at Best Service Hotel, Chris noticed the charter that read:

> *A customer is the most important person to ever enter our hotel.*
> *Though a customer may not be dependent on us, we are dependent*
> *on him or her.*

A well-presented Receptionist greeted the new guests with a warm smile and immediately led them to a pleasant seating area, offered them some complimentary refreshment and took brief check-in details from them. Asking to be excused for a few moments, she soon returned with a colleague from guest relations who was about to take them to their rooms when a familiar face approached Chris.

'It's good to see you again,' Support said. 'And good to see you in much finer spirits than when we first met in the Pub of Procrastination during my visit to a client in Mediocrity.'

For just a moment Chris did not recognise the person who had helped him when he most needed it.

'Of course!' he said. 'If it were not for you I would probably have lost my ambition to leave Apathy for ever.'

'You were always destined to come here,' replied Support. 'For you carried such a large Burden of frustration with you that your only hope was to take the action that you, your family and your colleagues thought so drastic at the time. Indeed we must each take whatever Burden we carry as an indication that we must do what is important to us and make the necessary changes in our lives.'

'Well, I've certainly done that,' said Chris. 'Indeed, having that Burden was more of a blessing in disguise than I realised.'

'And now that you are here, I would like to invite you to allow me to be of further service to you,' said Support. 'As soon as I heard that you had arrived I came over from my bank to meet with you. For at our bank we like to invest in winners and the basis of our criteria is a person's character. For we believe if you invest in character, what better collateral could there be? No document can ever replace integrity, no matter how well worded.'

'You're a banker?' enquired Chris. 'And you want to invest in me?'

'You and your team, in fact,' replied Support. 'I have followed your progress with interest, having spoken with Accountability, Probity and Innovate, even one of my colleagues, Attentive, who is currently advising in the State of Limbo. You have evaluated your motives and know what is important to you. Enthusiasm, Persistence and Discipline have reported that your mettle, steadfastness and sequential industry are more than what they could hope for, and Inspiration told me that you have a noble mission supported by values. And, as a team, I understand that you have already developed your strategy and customer ethos. What more could an investor want? Except Opportunity perhaps. And he has already confirmed that he will spend as much time with you as you require.'

Stunned, Chris and his colleagues just looked at each other. What Support had said made everything fall into place and be worthwhile. The three of them had shared so much together in their journey to Prosperity that, even though they were at the brink of realising all of their dreams, they found it hard to believe.

'Such rewards for my endeavour did not seem *possible* when I first started out,' said Chris. 'Yet, the *possibilities* that now exist are endless. Meeting up with Self-Reliance, after so many years, and working with Spontaneity has changed my outlook on so many things. I came in search of how to give better-than-excellent service and received greater-than-expected rewards!'

To Be a Pilgrim ...

- Understand that successful service is founded on personal commitment
- Know artificial procedures cannot replace attentive, friendly, reliable service
- Think like a self-employed entrepreneur, not a hired hand
- Be neither timid nor cavalier at whatever you do
- Being reliable is the best way to build a trusting relationship
- Believe that what is important to you warrants reward
- Never discriminate because of title or status
- Remember that the Law of Service promises you will always be rewarded in life in exact proportion to the value of your service to others
- The Law of *Enlightened* Service promises that you will always receive in life greater-than-expected rewards in consideration for how you have treated others
- Such rewards may not always come from where you thought, or at the time hoped. Yet they will *always* come and will *always* be greater than expected

Epilogue

The view from the terrace was spectacular. So was lunch and so was the service. It was consistently the case at Best Hotel. But today was made even more special for the first two diners who had arrived, because they were celebrating an anniversary.

'Well, we've certainly all benefited from your courage and determination,' said Christine. 'But by far the best thing, apart from living in Prosperity these past two years, of course, has been living with you *without* your Burden of Frustration. And it's so good to have the children settled at a school where they're praised for their strengths and are encouraged to develop empathy and consideration for others, while being motivated to release their potential.'

'I once commented to Self-Reliance how much I wanted to send my children to a school where they would be taught how to be the best they can be, rather than to get by how they can,' replied Chris. 'But by far the best thing for me has been being able to share what has been so important to me with the ones I love. Leaving you and going on that "business holiday", as you suggested, was the hardest thing that I have ever done.'

'I knew that it was at the time, but just consider where we would be if you had not done so? Still living in Mediocrity, *still* frustrated and *still* putting up with unsatisfactory service.'

'True, but you were the one who suggested my "retreat", in preference to taking the drastic action of resigning,' said Chris. 'But then you were proved right because if I had resigned I would have severed any relationship with my old colleagues and not have been able to help them.'

'Exactly, whereas now you have been able to help them with your ideas of Enlightened Service, drive your own organisation and develop a strategic alliance with them,' added Christine.

'Yes, since the company agreed to become a learning service organisation it has undergone quite a cultural change. Too-Busy is so much more focused and able to prioritise that everyone refers to him as Effective. And Cynical is the best ambassador an organisation could hope for. And all this because they took a "business holiday" themselves. He now has the reputation of Respected. Strange how the strongest opponent to change and to providing good service can become the strongest advocate, once he is able to change his perceptions about life.'

'But whatever did happen to Hidden-Agenda?' asked Christine.

'Well, when it looked fairly certain that the new ethos of the company was going to be fully bought into by everyone involved, his commitment seem to fall by the wayside. He didn't like our friends at Integrity House and chose to leave during a session there. The last I heard was that he had set up in a partnership with Rationale in Superficial Town, where life is apparently very much to his choosing.'

'Don't mention that place, it'll make me lose my appetite!' Self-Reliance quipped as he sat down. 'Though it does remind me, we received a message today at the office from a former travelling companion.'

'Impulsiveness?' asked Chris.

'The very same, except he has changed his name to Prepared since recently leaving the State of Chaos, and is now planning a journey towards Prosperity. Currently, he is working in the Zone of Enterprise with a former bankrupt, in a very successful business called Sequential Service. Apparently it's named after some symbol that hangs in the foyer of the building.'

'A shield,' put in Chris thoughtfully. 'It will be a shield and it means that the founder has successfully passed through the dark night of the soul.'

'Here I am,' said Spontaneity. 'With good news! Customer has just awarded us with his loyalty for another year. He really is our best ambassador, you know, so we must think of something really special this time to reward *him* for his patronage.'

'And we must also think of something a little different to surprise our own ambassadors who work with us, to reward *them* for developing the relationships that they have with all of our customers,' added Chris. 'The way they have turned so many one-time buyers into what will clearly be lifetime partners has been excellent! You know, just the other day I heard our training manager, Vocation, praise some new recruits for treating their very first customers as if they were lifetime customers who bought from us everyday!'

'Having been Redundant was a very valuable experience for Vocation, because he has so much empathy for everyone,' said Self-Reliance. 'He really believes in the importance of personal development as a precursor for learning how to give better-than-excellent service, and exemplifies his beliefs with his own performance towards his trainees. He literally treats them like his best customers.'

'And raises, appraises and praises them!' added Spontaneity.

Chris raised his glass. 'So let's drink our first toast to our customers, both external and *internal*. They are the reason that Communication Unlimited exists!'

Later that afternoon Chris took the opportunity to walk through the park on his way back to the office.

'So, how do you feel after two years doing what you love?' said Intuition.

'The very same as I did on the very first day I arrived,' replied Chris. 'Enthusiastic, eager and secure in following what I stand for.'

'When you make it a habit to improve yourself, the kind of world you want to inhabit swiftly follows doesn't it?' said Intuition. 'When you commit yourself to living the life you want, providence will always assist in achieving your destiny. For it cannot deny you. It can only reward you for your endeavours.'

'Providence has indeed assisted me, but it has been your guidance that has directed me,' said Chris. 'I just wish that I had learned to listen to it sooner. Perhaps, if I had not been weighed down with so much frustration, I would have been able to take action earlier.'

'Not at all. Your Burden was the very catalyst to stimulate change in your life. Remember that your frustration was brought on because you were fed up with living in mediocrity and having to put up with apathetic service. You felt certain that there must be an alternative, but had no idea in which direction to go to resolve it. Undertaking your journey allowed you to resolve your purpose, develop your mission and learn how to align what was important to you with your vocation. You became more receptive to my words because you were *ready* for them. You were looking for an answer to where your life was going. Prior to that, you did not consider there was any need, for you were following a path that was successful in comparison to others.

'It's true,' said Chris. 'I compared myself to others, little realising that genuine success comes from what I choose to do with my *own* potential in my life.'

'With half of life spelled "if", and half of success spelling "excess", is it any wonder that the journey of both is fraught with difficulty?' replied Intuition. 'Is it also any wonder that with our formative years teaching us how to get by, rather than how to get, the cry of *"What shall I do?"* is silently repeated by each of us more than any other phrase? Is it really any wonder that the majority of people dwell unwittingly in a world of mediocrity? A world where providing service is mistakenly interpreted as being servile and having customers is viewed as necessary, rather than important. A state where increasingly the other cry is *"what shall I do to be served?"*

'Having embarked on a personal journey of increased awareness and gained the reward of prosperity through enlightened service, I think that it is *no wonder* that there are such cries,' replied Chris. 'Indeed I believe that it is good that there are such questions raised. What is *not* good is that so many of us allow such questions to go unanswered, when all that is required is to *be* a pilgrim.'

COLIN TURNER

SHOOTING THE MONKEY
Secrets of the New Business Spirit

'As I am convinced that the key to long term business success is a secure philosophical and ethical background, I was delighted to read Colin Turner's latest book' *Sir John Harvey-Jones*

'Hooks like a thriller you can't put down ... That a book can succeed in being authoritative about management, success, business, lifestyle and spirituality is impressive. That it's also engrossing, inspiring and upbeat makes it essential reading for everyone with a job' *Time Out*

Shooting the Monkey shakes the very pillars of current thinking and business practice. With esoteric secrets, enlightening stories and insightful teachings, its twelve provocative scrolls present the forgotten alchemy essential to success, meaning and purpose in our evolving world.

After discovering the power of this new business spirit, your working life will never be the same again.

HODDER AND STOUGHTON PAPERBACKS

COLIN TURNER

SWIMMING WITH PIRANHA MAKES YOU HUNGRY
How to Simplify Your Life and Achieve
Financial Independence

'Brilliant!' *Daily Mail*

'Highly recommended' *Financial Times*

'Sound advice' *Sunday Independent*

'A thinking person's *Little Book of Calm*' *Belfast Telegraph*

Swimming With Piranha Makes You Hungry is a metaphorical must for anyone desiring to ensure their long-term security.

This unique book provides the powerful and practical advice essential for those seeking to enjoy life more, work less and *have more money!*

· Learn the laws vital for financial independence

· Discover the secrets to saving money

· Streamline your home, work, lifestyle and health

· Recognise new opportunities every day

Swimming With Piranha Makes You Hungry is guaranteed to improve the quality of your life

HODDER AND STOUGHTON PAPERBACKS

COLIN TURNER

MADE FOR LIFE
A Compelling Story of the Human Spirit's Quest for Fulfilment

'Why did you kill yourself?'

It was the second time the voice had asked the question. The man did not want to answer, but the words came anyway.

'What else could I have done?'

In this classic tale of wisdom, an individual struggles for understanding and guidance in his quest for a definite meaning and purpose in life. MADE FOR LIFE reveals the secret of success and is a perfect guide to finding fulfilment.

Everyone will benefit from reflecting on the deep, life-changing ideas that fill its pages, because it is impossible not to relate to its meaningful message.

'The most exciting and unique book I have ever read and most of it delivers a very important message. You will love it' *Uri Geller*

'If you are looking for answers in your spiritual life – this little book speaks volumes' *Stuart Wilde*

'*Made for Life* is an excellent guide for making your life work, maybe one could even call it the philosophy for the 21st century. It should be required reading' *Vera Peiffer*

'A profound, contemplative and meaningful story' *Dr Wayne W Dyer*

'An irresistible read. This book doesn't just raise the questions in oneself, it actually provides the answers!' *Alan Cohen*

'I doubt very much whether anyone's life will remain unchanged after reading it' *Here's Health*

HODDER AND STOUGHTON PAPERBACKS